Praise for *The Hilliker Curse*

'Grimly fascinating ... shines a spotlight on Ellroy's "wildly passionate quest for atonement in women" ... This self portrait of the artist as a man almost pathologically sexually arrested in early adolescence makes for a seductive, uncomfortable, at times ugly, but always unputdownable read.'

Evening Standard

'James Ellroy's crime novels have been much acclaimed for their dark plots, tough prose and generally bleak view of the world. Now that he's brought those same qualities to bear on a history of relationships with women, the result, inevitably, is not for the faint-hearted ... Ellroy writes with such swagger and certainty that it's hard not to be swept along. He also – let's face it – has quite a tale to tell.'

Daily Mail

'A remarkable memoir ... Hugely enjoyable.'

The Economist

'*The Hilliker Curse* is a biography of obsession. It continually circles and revisits the author's compulsions and addictions ... He directs the bullet prose at himself and pushes the persona factor into the red ... He wears his Oedipal complex like a garish shirt, professing his truth – especially the ugly truth – with a bravado that dares us to still love him in the morning ... There's something compelling about a writer like Ellroy operating out of his comfort zone ... He's never boring. We turn the pages gripped with a rubbernecker's fascination ... It is ugly, beautiful, reprehensible and moving. In other words, a hard book to forget. Ellroy speaks to and for the obsessive creep in every man. At high volume.'

Irish Times

'In *The Hilliker Curse*, the master of American crime fiction chooses not to dwell on his triumphs. Instead, he mines his dark ego, and creeps from the pages as a pervert, a peeping tom, a john, an addict, a mother-fantasist, a hypochondriac and a sociopath ... The terse, noirish style of his crime thrillers does not desert him here.'

Sunday Times

'High-octane ... A breathless piece of writing ... When it comes to pinning down the most startling possible word collision, Ellroy's acrobatic pizzazz is beyond doubt ... This is literary knife-throwing at its most exhilarating and dangerous ... An impassioned love letter written by a man who does at least sincerely believe he has now found The One.'

Guardian

'Writing with ferocious scope and a brutally clipped prose style, Ellroy is a profane, slangy gatecrasher to the league of Serious American Novelists ... His foul-mouthed, condensed style has a certain purpose. It chimes perfectly with his bleak historical worldview ... His writing is deliberately hellish.'

Financial Times

'A painfully honest book, written in Ellroy's usual blunt, breathless but often starkly beautiful prose ... A monument to the author as compassionate lover, intellectual giant, creative powerhouse and emotional truthteller. It's a marvellous read, sly, self-mocking and filled with troubling insight.'

Time Out

'The latest from this American literary legend is a stark rendition of murder, nervous breakdown, affairs, divorces and much more. It's an incredibly frank and soul-bearing piece of writing which goes some way to explaining the extreme and obsessive nature of Ellroy's brilliant novels.'

Big Issue

'Riveting ... As you might expect from the author of The Black Dahlia and LA Confidential, this is the most addictive of reads about life, love and self-discovery, in astonishing, soul-baring detail. An unforgettable autobiography.'

Red

The Hilliker Curse

My Pursuit of Women

JAMES ELLROY

WINDMILL BOOKS

Published by Windmill Books 2011

2 4 6 8 10 9 7 5 3 1

Copyright © James Ellroy 2010

James Ellroy has asserted his right under the Copyright, Designs and
Patents Act, 1988, to be identified as the author of this work.

Portions of this work previously appeared in slightly different form in *Playboy*.

First published in Great Britain in 2010 by William Heinemann

Windmill Books
The Random House Group Limited
20 Vauxhall Bridge Road, London SW1V 2SA

Addresses for companies within The Random House Group Limited can be found at:
www.randomhouse.co.uk/offices.htm

The Random House Group Limited Reg. No. 954009

www.randomhouse.co.uk

A CIP catalogue record for this book
is available from the British Library

ISBN 9780099537854

The Random House Group Limited supports The Forest Stewardship
Council (FSC), the leading international forest certification organisation.
All our titles that are printed on Greenpeace approved FSC certified paper
carry the FSC logo. Our paper procurement policy can be found at:
www.randomhouse.co.uk/environment

Mixed Sources
Product group from well-managed
forests and other controlled sources
www.fsc.org Cert no. TT-COC-002139
© 1996 Forest Stewardship Council

Printed and bound in Great Britain by
CPI Bookmarque Ltd, Croydon, CR0 4TD

To Erika Schickel

I will take Fate by the throat.

—LUDWIG VAN BEETHOVEN

So women will love me.

I invoked The Curse a half century ago. It defines my life from my tenth birthday on. The near-immediate results have kept me in near-continuous dialogue and redress. I write stories to console her as a phantom. She is ubiquitous and never familiar. Other women loom flesh and blood. They have their stories. Their touch has saved me in varying increments and allowed me to survive my insane appetite and ambition. They have withstood my recklessness and predation. I have resisted their rebukes. My storytelling gifts are imperviously strong and rooted in the moment that I wished her dead and mandated her murder. Women give me the world and hold the world tenuously safe for me. I cannot go to Them to find Her much longer. My obsessive will is too stretched. Their story must eclipse Hers in volume and content. I must honor Them and distinguish each one from Her. My pursuit has been both raw and discerning. The latter comforts me now. There were always grace notes in with the hunger.

It's been a fever dream. I must decorously decode it. They are all gone now. I'm unbodied without them. If I address them with candor, they'll cut me loose of the fury. My grasp may recede to a touch in retrospect. I'll find the answer in dreams and waking flashes. They'll find me alone and talk to me in the dark.

PART I

HER

1

The numbers don't matter. It's not a body count, a scratch-pad list or a boast. Statistics obscure intent and meaning. My toll is therefore ambiguous. Girlfriends, wives, one-night stands, paid companions. Chaste early figures. A high-stat blitz later on. Quantity means shit in my case. Culminated contact means less than that. I was a watcher at the get-go. Visual access meant capture. The Curse incubated my narrative gift. My voyeur's eye pre-honed it. I lived a kiddie version of my twisted heroes thirty years hence.

We're looking. We're eyeball-arched and orbing in orbit. We're watching women. We want something enormous. My heroes don't know it yet. Their virginal creator has not a clue. We don't know that we're reading personae. We're looking so that we can stop looking. We crave the moral value of one woman. We'll know Her when we see Her. In the meantime, we'll look.

A document denotes my early fixation. It's dated 2/17/55. It predates The Curse by three years. It's a playground shot in Kodak black & white.

A jungle gym, two slides and a sandbox clutter the foreground. I'm standing alone, stage left. I'm lurchlike big and unkempt. My upheaval is evident. A stranger would mark me as a fucked-up child in everyday duress. I have beady eyes. They're fixed on four girls, huddled stage right. The photo is rife with objects and children in lighthearted movement. I'm coiled in pure study. My scrutiny is staggeringly intense. I'll re-read my mind from 55 years back.

These four girls bode as The Other. I'm a pious Lutheran boy. There can be only one. Is it her, her, her or Her?

I think my mother took the picture. A neutral parent would have cropped out the freako little boy. Jean Hilliker at 39: the pale skin and red hair, center-parted and tied back—my features and fierce eyes and a sure grace that I have never possessed.

The photo is a windowsill carving. I was still too young to roam unfettered and press my face up to the glass. My parents split the sheets later that year. Jean Hilliker got primary custody. She put my dad on skates and rolled him to a cheap pad a few blocks away. I snuck out for quick visits. High shrubs and drawn shades blocked my views en route. My mother told me that my father was spying on her. She sensed it. She said she saw smudge marks on her bedroom window. I read the divorce file years later. My father copped out to peeping. He said he peeped to indict my mother's indigenous moral sloth.

He saw her having sex with a man. It did not legally justify his presence at her window. Windows were beacons. I knew it in my crazed-child rush to The Curse. I entered houses through windows a decade hence. I never left smudge marks. My mother and father taught me that.

She had the stones. He had the bunco-artist gab and the grin. She always worked. He dodged work and schemed like Sergeant Bilko and the Kingfish on *Amos 'n' Andy*. The pastor at my church called him the "world's laziest white man."

He had a sixteen-inch schlong. It dangled out of his shorts. All his friends talked about it. This is not a whacked-out child's reconstruction.

Jean Hilliker got bourbon-bombed and blasted the Brahms concertos. Armand Ellroy subscribed to scandal rags and skin magazines. I got two days a week with him. He let me stare out his front window and fuck with his binoculars. My ninth birthday arrived. My mother got me a new church suit. My dad asked me what I wanted. I said I wanted a pair of X-ray eyeglasses. I saw them advertised in a comic book.

He yukked and said, Okay. He sent a buck in through the U.S. mail. My wait was grindingly attenuated. I made lists of all the school and church girls that I could see naked. I concocted ways to tape the glasses to my toy periscope. It would provide instant window access.

I waited—March, April, May, '57. Late spring through the summer. I couldn't track the sale. I had to trust the manufacturer's honor and efficacy.

The wait derailed my fantasy life. I spun out in new directions. I sat in my mother's clothes closet. I loved the smell of her lingerie and nurse's uniforms. I swiped my dad's binoculars and spied on a neighbor lady. I saw her reach under her blouse and pluck at her bra strap.

Fall '57. The Long Wait. Mickey Spillane wrote a book with that title. Spillane was the king of the anti-Commie thriller. My dad had a special shelf for his Spillane tomes. He said I could read them on my tenth birthday.

It's the Season of My Discombobulation. It's winging into the Withering Winter of My Dipshit Discontent. I was agitated. The TV news scared me. The Russians launched *Sputnik*. Colored kids caused chaos at Central High School. I was dreading Christmas. My mother had sched-uled a trip to Madison, Wisconsin. We were going to see her sister. Aunt Leoda married a Catholic. My dad thought she was Red.

The X-ray eyeglasses arrived.

My dad forked them over. I unwrapped the package and put them on. I squinted through colored cellophane. I peered around our living room. It was tinted turquoise.

The walls didn't melt. I couldn't see the crisscrossed beams under the plaster. My dad laughed at me. Sandra Danner's house was three blocks away. I sprinted there, full tilt.

Sandy and her mom were up stringing Christmas lights. I put my glasses on and stared at them. They laughed at me. Sandy touched her head and twirled a finger. It was '50s-speak for *He Craaaaazy.*

The glasses were a shuck. I knew about confidence schemes from *Whisper* magazine. Hucksters sold elderly stiffs plutonium mines in the Alps. They bilked the old cocksuckers and sent them to the poorhouse. I ripped the glasses into shreds of cardboard and cellophane. Sandy Danner went *He Craaaaazy* again. Her mom offered me a cookie.

I ran back to the pad. My dad was still laughing. He gave me my consolation prize: a new baseball. I chucked it out the window. My dad yukked and told me to shake a leg. We were going to a movie up in Hollywood. My flight east was that night.

The flick was called *Plunder Road.* Psycho losers loot a train loaded with gold bullion. Two of the guys had zaftig blond girlfriends. They wore tight blouses and pedal pushers. The theater was near empty. I moved closer for a better orb on the chicks. My dad lobbed Jordan almonds at my head and chortled.

The heist went bad. The Main Loser and the Main Blonde welded the bullion to the front bumper of her car and chrome-plated it. They headed out to T.J. on the Holly-wood Freeway. Malign fate intervened. The Main Loser and Main Blonde got in a fender bender. An alert cop noticed the gold underplating and wasted the Main Loser's ass. The Main Blonde pitched some boo-hoo. Her big chi-chis shook.

The movie spooked me. My wig was loose. I didn't want to fly to Dogdick, Wisconsin. My dad strolled me down Hollywood side streets and cut north on Cherokee. He installed me on the front steps of a building. He said he'd be inside for an hour. He gave me a comic book and said, Don't roam.

I was a dirty-minded child with a religious streak. My shit detector clicked in, resultantly. My mom told a friend that my dad craved skirt action. I heard my dad use the term *fuck pad*. I concluded this: He's porking the Main Blonde from the movie.

I noticed a half-full jug of cheap wine by the mailbox bank. I guzzled it and got goofy and euphoric. I'm tanked. I go window-peeping.

Cherokee north of the Boulevard. Spanish apartment houses and bungalow courts. Windows ringed with Christ-mas lights. Low first-floor windowsills. Perch spots for a tall little boy hot to LOOK.

I was blitzed. It was 53 years ago. I know I didn't see the Main Blonde or my dad in the saddle. I know I saw a fat guy flipping burgers. I know I saw a skinny lady watching TV.

It all blurred then. Booze blackout—age nine.

I recall a queasy cab ride. I'm back at my mom's pad in Santa Monica. I'm in my church suit. We're on an airplane. Jean Hilliker's wearing a blue serge dress and holding an overcoat. Her red hair is cinched by a tortoiseshell barrette. She's drinking a highball and smoking a cigarette.

I leaned close. She misunderstood my intent and ruffled

my hair. I wanted to nuzzle her and taste the bourbon. She didn't know that.

I dozed off. Jean Hilliker dozed off. I woke up and watched her sleep. She was 42 now. She was boozing more. It showed on her face. She went back to Hilliker, post-divorce decree. It stigmatized me. Her pride, my bifurcated identity. I killed off the dregs of her highball and ate the cherry. It gave me a residual jolt. I saw a woman enter a lavatory at the rear of the plane.

I traipsed over and perched near the door. Passing adults ignored me. Women used the facility. I hovered and heard the door locks click. The women exited and scowled at me. I read biblical censure on their faces. One woman forgot to lock the door. I barged in accidentally on purpose. The woman shrieked. I saw sheer nylon stockings and some skin.

Madison, Wisconsin, was lake-bound and penguin-shit cold. A snow-covered field flanked Aunt Leoda's house. I got into a snowball fight the first day. An ice-crusted ball busted up my face and loosened some wobbly teeth. I holed up in a back bedroom and brooded.

My cousins were off being happy kids at Christmas. Jean Hilliker was off with plain-Jane Aunt Leoda and porky Uncle Ed. Uncle Ed sold Buicks. My mother purchased a red-and-white sedan from him. The plan: drive the fucker back to L.A. after New Year's.

I brooded. The practice entailed long stints alone in the dark. I thought about girls then. I brain-screened girls I'd seen at school and at church. It was a pure visual panoply. I did not impose story lines. I have formally brooded through to this moment. I lie in the dark, shut my eyes and think. I think about women primarily. I quite often tremble and sob. My heart swells in sync with women's faces merged with improvised stories. History intercedes. Great public events run counterpoint to deep human love. Women glimpsed for half seconds carry a spiritual weight equal to my long-term lovers.

Bumfuck, Wisconsin, was a drag. My mouth hurt. The fucking snowball sliced my lips. I couldn't kiss Christine Nelson from school. My dad said he knew a TV babe named Chris Nelson. She was married to a Hebe named Louie Quinn. Chris was a nympho. She flashed her snatch at him at some movie-biz party.

The adults came home. My mother brought me a library book. It was wholesome kids' fare, full of mystical shit. It pertained to witchcraft, spells and curses. My mother turned the bedroom lights on. I had to read rather than brood.

The book jazzed me. I tore through it quicksville. It felt like it was written for me. The mystical jive derived from my ancestral home of Shitsville, Great Britain. Magic potions abounded. Warlocks guzzled secret brews and had visions. This wowed the incipient boozehound and dope fiend in me. The overall text buttressed religious lore I believed in then and believe in today.

There's a world we can't see. It exists separately and concurrently with the real world. You enter this world by the offering of prayer and incantation. You live in this world wholly within your mind. You dispel the real world through mental discipline. You rebuff the real world through your enforced mental will. Your interior world will give you what you want and what you need to survive.

I believed it then. I believe it now. My many years in the dark have confirmed it as a primary article of faith. I was nine then. I'm 62 now. The real world has frequently intruded on my spells in the dark. That book formally sanctioned me to lie still and conjure women. I did it then. I do it still. That book described the destructive power of formal invective. The notion of The Curse did not feel prophetic in late 1957. It was simply a footnote to my license to fantasize.

I have a superbly honed memory. My time in the dark has enhanced my process of minutely detailed recollection. My mental ruthlessness asserted itself early on.

I needed a Curse a few months later. I was insolently well prepared.

The new Buick was a full-dress road hog. It had wide whites and more chrome than the *Plunder Road* death sled. I wanted to zoom it back to L.A. and see my dad. I wanted to resume my fantasy life back on my home turf.

The adults went nightclubbing on New Year's Eve. A German immigrant girl baby-sat my cousins and me. She was 17 or 18, acne-addled and plump. She wore a reindeer blouse and a flannel skirt with a pink embroidered poodle. She emitted Hitler-Jugend vibes.

She tucked me in last. The bedroom door was shut. Her fluttery presence felt un-kosher. She sat on the edge of the bed and patted me. The vibe devolved. She pulled down the covers and sucked my dick.

I dug it and recoiled from it in equal measure. I withstood thirty seconds and pushed her off. She talked a Kraut blue streak and bolted the room. I killed the lights and brooded out the bad juju.

I felt sideswiped, more than assaulted. I recalled the magic-spell book. I figured I could brew a blank-memory elixir. I could create X-ray eye powder at the same time. I got bilked on those glasses. My secret eyeball blend would set that straight.

I fell asleep in '57 and woke up in '58. Jean Hilliker and I split Madison in snow flurries. It worsened a few hours in. We crossed the Iowa border. The road froze. The snow turned to ice. My mother pulled over and bundled me in the backseat. Cars lost traction and brodied on the highway. Wheels slid on slick blacktop. Low-speed collisions multiplied. Fool drivers smoked their tires down to bare tread and skittered into cornfields.

Jean Hilliker *winked* at me. She was *performing*. I've got the entire sequence freeze-framed. She wore a tartan scarf over her hair and a brown overcoat. She pulled back onto the road.

I watched. She chain-smoked as she maneuvered. She worked the pedals in her stocking feet and gained ground in low gear. Cars caromed, bumped and rolled backward all around us. Jean rode the slow lane and sliced mud with her right tires. Ice shards bombarded the windshield. Jean ran the defroster and melted the ice on contact. The car was steam-room hot. Jean ditched her overcoat. She wore a short-sleeved blue blouse underneath it. I noticed how pale and lovely her arms were.

We skidded in and out of mud troughs. We clipped rural fence posts and sheared off our right sideview mirror. Jean scanned the road for no-ice patches. She stayed ahead of back-sliding cars and kept her eyes peeled for new ones. She gripped the steering wheel loosely and braced it with her left knee. She smoked cigarettes, white-knuckled.

The weather shifted. The ice mulched and set the road traversable. We turned into an auto court and got a room for the night. It featured timber walls inset with plaster moldings. My mother found a string quartet on the radio. We were sweat-soaked from her boffo play with the defroster. I showered first and put on pajamas.

She felt different that night. She overtook my dad within

my crazy heart for a moment. Her eyes were tight and gray-flecked some new way. She had smiled and went "Oops" every time she banged a mailbox.

I pretended to sleep. She walked out of a steam cloud and toweled herself off, naked. I slitted my eyes and memorized her body for the ten zillionth time. She never hid her nakedness. She never flaunted it. She was a registered nurse. Her nakedness was always deadpan working on brusque. She was a woman of science and undoubtedly equated sex with cellular function. She wanted me to ask her the facts-of-life questions. She wanted to vouch her stance as an enlightened mother and the first Hilliker to attend college. I didn't want abstract responses. I wanted to know about Her and sex in an enticing manner with a mystical bent. I wanted God and Her and her separate world in perfect proportion.

I had seen her in flagrante before. This geek Hank Hart was her first post-divorce squeeze. I got some of the mechanics down and stood back from the doorway. Hank Hart had lost a thumb in a drill-press mishap. My mother had lost the tip of one nipple to a post-childbirth infection. I skimmed the Bible and my dad's scandal rags for a sex-with-missing-body-parts parlay. I got adultery condemned and Sinuendo. I went back to eyeballing women for my answers.

We cleared the storm zone the next day and turned right in Texas. I scoped out girls in passing cars and scratched my balls on the sly. My mother said we might move in February. She was hipped to a house in the San Gabriel Valley. Our gelt was running thin. We were splurging on cheeseburgers and rustic motels. The Buick slurped high-test gas through four fat carburetors. We laid up in Albuquerque and went to a movie. It was a seagoing turkey called *Fire Down Below*. The stars: Robert Mitchum, Jack Lemmon and Rita Hayworth.

I pointed to Hayworth's name on the screen. My mother *glared* at it. My dad went back to the '30s with *La Roja Rita*. It pre-dated his circa '40 hookup with Jean. Rita was half Anglo, half Mex aristocrat. My dad was working as a croupier in T.J. Rita's father hired him to watchdog Rita and deter mashers. My dad told me that he poured Rita the pork. I cannot verify this assertion. My dad *did* enjoy a long run as Rita's chief stooge. Rita sacked his lazy ass, circa '50.

My parents defied easy classification. Jean Hilliker hit L.A. in late '38. She won a beauty contest, tanked a screen test and returned to Chicago. She lived in a big pad with four other nurses. A beefy bull dyke ruled the roost. Jean got pregnant, tried to scrape herself and hemorrhaged. A doctor chum undid the damage. She had an affair with him, dumped him and married a rich stiff. Marriage #1 fizzled pronto. Jean remembered how good L.A. looked and caught a bus. A friend knew a ginch named Jean Feese. Jean F. was wed to a hunky drifter named Ellroy.

They met, they sizzled, they shacked. My dad dumped Jean #1. Jean #2 got pregnant in '47. They got married in August. A troubled pregnancy foretold my rapturously troubled and memoir-mapped life.

I never *got* Rita Hayworth. She was plucked, lacquered, varnished, depilatoried, injected and enhanced. She shit-canned my dad before the Hilliker-Ellroy marriage imploded. She was my dad's defaulting deus ex machina. He had a sweet deal with Rita. She blew it—not him. There were more sweet deals ahead. Other Ritas were out there. He would glom himself one.

It was loser shtick to a dipshit child predisposed to believe it. I heard it expressed plaintively, whiningly and disingenuously. Jean Hilliker heard it shrieked, sobbed and bellowed—behind bedroom doors closed to me. She under-estimated my ability to eavesdrop and extrapolate. She did not credit me with a knack for decoding sighs. She went at my father with less volume and pathos. I watched her sadness and fury build from the inside out. I never *heard* her say it. I watched her think it and suppress it from the outside in.

You're weak. You live off of women. I won't let you take much more of me.

I knew it was true—then.

I sided with him—then.

I hated her then. I hated her because *he* was *me* and once he was gone I'd be alone with the breadth of my shame. I hated her because I wanted her in unspeakable ways.

I was an Ellroy then. I'm a Hilliker now. *Our* pride, my bifurcated identity.

My father made me his co-defiler. His mantra was, *She's a drunk and a whore.* I cravenly acceded to the dictum. He told me he had private eyes tailing my mother. I believed it then. I know it was hoo-ha now. It didn't matter then. *Cherchez la femme.* The imagined detectives led me to women.

All solitary men were detectives. All male pedestrians were detectives. All men hiding behind newspapers were specifically tailing me. My dad employed at least one whole detective agency. An equal number of gumshoes were stalking my mother.

My father was out discovering the next Rita Hayworth. His job description was "Film-Biz Slave" and "Hollywood Bottom-Feeder." He was tapping some fantasy windfall. He scored the big bowl of bread that Sergeant Bilko and the Kingfish fell short of in pratfalls and greed. Private fuzz ran pricey. My dad loved me *that* much. A flatfoot fleet safeguarded me. Fleet #2 tailed the round-heeled redhead to juke joints and hot-sheet motels. Moral turpitude was a tough sell. Kiddie-court judges usually sided with the mom. My dad had film-biz clout. He had the lowdown on bribable Jew judges. He just slipped Perry Mason a fat retainer.

That wowed me. I watched *Perry Mason* every week. My case might wind up on TV.

My school was on Wilshire and Yale. My pad was off Broadway and Princeton. Santa Monica had semi-brisk foot traffic. I walked to school most days and dawdled home indirectly. My roaming range was two miles in circumference. Wilshire was dotted with cocktail caves and auto courts. I grooved the Broken Drum, the Fox and Hounds, and the Ivanhoe. I loitered outside and watched the detectives enter and split. I gave them perfunctory glances and shifted my gaze to any and all nearby women. I confirmed that my dad's goons were on the job and went wild with the adjoining scenery.

It's a fifty-year-old blur in '50s film-process color. It's etched in VistaVision and Sinerama. There're stop frames and jump cuts that signify new stimuli and depict my divided attention.

Some details remain ripe. Uni High coeds pour off the Wilshire bus. One girl dangles her schoolbooks, cinched by a brown belt. I side-tail a chubby girl. She's bare-armed. One dress strap keeps falling, she keeps retrieving it. She's got dark stubble, all powder-flecked. I watch women enter rooms at the Ivanhoe. One woman is Italianate and picks at her stocking runs. Bus stops were good spots for repeat eyeball business. I saw the same detective at Santa Monica and Franklin several times. He was always chatting with a neighbor lady. She wore a dark green dress one day and showed boocoo back. The zipper was stuck above her bra strap. She told the man she worked in Beverly Hills. She carried a briefcase instead of a purse. I placed her age as Jean Hilliker's age. She always smoked a last cigarette and dropped it ahead of the right-front bus wheel.

I waited for her one evening. I was *nine* years old and just that obsessed. The westbound bus dropped her across the street from the outgoing bus stop. I tailed her to a crib on

Arizona. She opened the door and saw me. She gave me a schizy look and shut the door. I never saw her again.

It was surveillance within surveillance. I breezed through coffee shops, used the can and breezed out. I entered lounge lairs verboten to children and eyeballed the bar. I saw women reflected in above-the-bar mirrors. I saw women twirl ashtrays and look pensive. I saw women dangle low-heeled shoes off one foot.

Samo High and Lincoln Junior High were close to my pad. Kids materialized on my block around 4:00 on school days. Boys and girls together. Older kids. The girls hugged their schoolbooks and swerved their breasts. One girl rested her chin on her books and swayed as she walked. She always lagged behind the other kids. She was pale. She had long dark hair and wore glasses. She lived one courtyard over from me. I didn't know her name. I decided to call her "Joan."

I spied on her bungalow. I saw her reading a few times. She sat in an easy chair crossways and wiggled her feet. I studied her family life. Her dad wore a Jew beanie and doted on her. Mom favored the doltish kid brother. I have thought about Joan and prayed for Joan for 53 continuous years. I considered her a prophet then. I was correct. The real-named woman Joan appeared 46 years later. She was that wish-named high school girl, physical point by physical point.

Both Joans are gone now. The real-named Joan had stunning gray-streaked hair. It's been four years since I've seen her. I heard she had a child. I wonder how much more gray has swirled through the black.

We made it back to L.A. on gas fumes and a buck-98. The Buick was paint-pocked and minus that right mirror. I returned to my roamings and ruminations. Jean Hilliker went back to bourbon and Brahms and her nurse gig at Airtek Dynamics.

I didn't think about the magic book or the Nazi chick and her aborted knob job. I didn't brew potions. I got pissed at my mother after church one cold morning. I told her to beware—my dad had hired Perry Mason to get custody of me. Jean Hilliker found this sidesplitting. She explained that Perry Mason was a TV fiction. Moreover: That beetle-browed actor's a swish.

The old man kept bugging me to spy on my mother. He kept calling the crib and driving her batshit. She kept bringing up the move to the suburbs.

She persisted, she insisted, she blathered, she cajoled, she lied. "The Suburbs": euphemism/propaganda/forked-tongue doublespeak. The San Gabriel Valley was blast-oven exile. Renegade rednecks and waterlogged wetbacks. A shit-kicker Shangri-la.

Of course, we moved there.

Of course, she died there.

Of course, I caused her death.

I throw myself at women and talk to them alone in the dark. They speak back to me. They have convinced me of my guilt.

We left right before Valentine's Day. I slid a card embossed with a big red heart under Joan's door. I bought the real-named Joan a Valentine's card and a blouse 48 years later. We made love in a hotel suite and planned our wedding.

It ended soon after. I'm alone with Joan imagery now. I'm mentally watching her age and grow stronger. She's inside me with all of the others, each and every one distinct.

2

My dad got me. He alleged fluke providence. He didn't
have to retain Perry Mason or bribe Jew judges. We were
both relieved and gratified. The murder went unsolved. I
dodged the issue of my guilt and breezed through a season
of adult solicitude. Nobody blamed me. *There, there.* Isn't
he brave and cute?

Alas, no.

Summer '58 unfurled smoggy and powder blue. I
stalked girls at Lemon Grove Park. I stole a chemistry set,
mixed powders randomly and sweetened my potions with
Kool-Aid. I watched the *Criswell Predicts* TV show devotedly. Criswell was a fruity guy with a cape. He foresaw the
future and spoke portentously. He exemplified the shuck of
self-confidence. I studied him and honed my act under this
boob-tube spell. The Mighty Ellroy has decreed: You will
drink this sacred elixir and disrobe!

The caustic chemicals outwafted the Kool-Aid. No girls
put their lips to my cups. I dodged murder-one indictments
again. Credit me with avant-garde panache. My shtick dramatically preceded the Jim Jones Massacre.

A nearby five-and-dime sold various brands of X-ray eye
glasses. I stole them all and tried them all and got nil results.
I bopped out to the Andrews Hardware Store. They sold

infrared binoculars for night hunters. *I was a skin hunter.* The binoculars were expensive and too big to swipe. I aimed them at female patrons and saw my clothed prey in a red haze. A few women laughed and patted my head. *Awwwww,* isn't he cute?

Alas, no.

I lived to read, brood, peep, stalk, skulk and fantasize. My reading focus zeroed in on kids' crime books and lingered there all summer. Rich kids from happy families solved murders. Ordered worlds got resurrected and nobody got too fucked-up. There were no Weegee-like photos. Homicide was sanitized. No semen stains, no blood spray. No locked-limb rigor mortis.

Formulaic pap. My sublimated dialogue on the Jean Hilliker snuff. Triage therapy that prepared me for Mickey Spillane.

Mike Hammer was a chick magnet and a Commie-snuff artiste. He pistol-whipped left-wingers and bit women's necks. He was dutifully dichotomized. He brutalized bad men and saved virtuous women. Mike Hammer's quest became my moral credo. There was one major sticking point that vexed me.

Not all women expressed virtue. Some women were shrill and usurious. One woman was really a man with an implied donkey dick. Society women were One-Worlders and Comsymps. Mike Hammer slapped bad women around. Mike Hammer shot the big-dick he/she in cold blood. I could not read those passages. I could not endure depictions of violence on women. The same dynamic held with TV and film fare. *I could not see it.* I had to shut my eyes. I banished hurt women from my purview. I insisted that my maimed women remain off-page and offscreen. It was a bedrock of empathy within my overall kiddie-noir predation.

Hurt women brought me back to Her. Mental tenacity kept my guilt suppressed. I was a sex-crazed little boy *before* the death I mandated. I tamped down the upshot now. The fount of my will was, and is, the ability to exploit misfortune. Puberty boded. My hormones hosannaed. The stimulus of All Women All The Time forced me to contain the obsession. I was already a seasoned brooder and watcher. I started telling myself stories to rein it in.

Savior-of-women fantasies. Romantic tableaux set against history. Mike Hammer sans misogynist text.

I got hopped up on the Black Dahlia murder case. Starstruck girl hits L.A. and winds up severed and dumped. It's another unsolved woman snuff. It's L.A. '47, again in SinemaScope.

I saved the Dahlia, alone in the dark. I killed her killer and resuscitated her with magic potions. I time-traveled. We dined at defunct hot spots resurrected from old photographs and impromptu imagery. We made love in a bungalow at the Beverly Hills Hotel. My dad and Rita Hayworth were our flunkies. They shagged us chow from Ollie Hammond's Steak House. I wasn't a skinny kid with emergent acne. I was Zachary Scott with that cool mustache and my dad's giant dick. The sexual mechanics were virgin-boy fantasia. A filtering process came and went and often shut down my narrative steam. I would see my mother in bed with Hank Hart. I would blot the image out and pray it away.

The Dahlia was a frequent co-star. I denied her martyred kinship with Jean Hilliker. A morbid subtext slammed me to Dahlialand. The same death sense shocked me and boomeranged me to my present-day world. I created stirring unions with local girls and their mothers.

I lived in a hotbox dive adjoining swank Hancock Park. Ritzy houses were arrayed in three directions. My dad and I owned a baleful beagle. She was dominant. She bit us and kept us in line. She defied housebreaking. She turned our pad into a dog-dung *demimonde*. The scent socked itself in and accreted. I took the dog for long late-night walks and peeped Hancock Park windows.

The girls went to posh private schools. They wore pastel uniform dresses by day and prepped-out civvies in the evenings. Madras shirtwaists and tartan kilts. Gingham button-downs inherited from big brothers. Sherbet-shade gowns for cotillions.

The girls were stunning in their collective pedigree. The girls were individually lovely as I peeped them in prosaic context. I had a secret compact with them. My access was God-like. It fueled my hunger and assuaged my privation in alternating heartbeats.

I took the girls home with me and talked to them in the dark. They spoke back to me in candid whispers. I concocted kid stories suffused with social-class struggle and love-conquers-all elation. My girls were never standard pretty or comely in prescribed ways. I was always looking for the physical flaw or distinction that marked gravity. I looked in window after window at face after face. I was looking for one face. There can be only one. Thus she will be me and she will be THE OTHER.

"The Other": My real self made whole by an image. My hurt salved by a loving female touch.

Voyeur. Pious Protestant boy. Fatuous seeker.

It played out *aaaaall* in my head.

I took the girls home. Their mothers found me and pushed me into walls, threw me down and *had* me. Their hunger was my hunger expressed through their haunted aggression. They squeezed my face. Their hands hurt me. Our mouths clashed. Our teeth scraped. Our nakedness was blurred by a shutter stop inside me. I was frail and

unequal to their bounty. It scared me then. The roughness
unhinged me. The absence of a narrative line left me
weightless. I didn't know what it meant *then*. I'll ascribe
meaning *now*. They wanted me because I sensed who they
were and went at them with that raging instinct. A dead
woman fed me the knowledge. They were indistinguishable
and each and every one unique. My moral intent was
gender-wide and paid for in blood—frail boy bound credi-
ble and ghastly deep.

Women were everywhere and nowhere. My dad hid his girlfriends. Our dog-shit dive deterred assignations there. I
overheard his "Hey, baby" calls and inferred fuck-pad
dates. He had no family. Jean Hilliker's kin were back in
Whipdick, Wisconsin. I went to school and church because
I had to and because there were women there. It got me out
of the dog den and into the fresh air. Human interaction
momentarily rewired my fantasy life. I was forced to sit, listen and talk. Matriculation led me to second-rung obsessions. American history and classical music started tearing
through me. They were subsidiary fixations. They momentarily fogged my all-women mind-set.

I co-opted them fast. My woman-savior tales took on
verisimilitude and topical oomph. Beethoven wrote me
scores. Our rhapsodies out-juiced the Ninth Symphony and
the late string quartets.

I *had* to talk to people. *All* people scared me. Women and
girls scared me much more than men and boys. I addressed
all males with braggadocio undercut with tight-throat fear. I
ducked my head, made provocative statements and cut in
and out of discourse quick. I could not talk to females
beyond non sequiturs. I flopped at talking *to* boys about
girls. Their chat was too graphic, too uninformed and jejune

without my puerile grandeur. I stayed pent-up into raging adolescence. Age ten to age thirteen was an onset-of-puberty blur. I grew tall and stayed commensurately unbodied. A neighbor boy introduced me to masturbation. I discovered it astoundingly late. That fact explicates my mental predisposition and horror of real sex. I reinvested sex and postponed approach every time I saw a female who might be The Other. I was a Scottish pastor's grandson and the scion of farmers and clergymen who took to the bottle instead of the flesh. I would have it all in due time and nearly die from it. My mind and soul met my right hand at age 13. It all accelerated. Jean Hilliker moldered in the backwash of fresh hand technique and constant stimuli.

Junior high was high-octane. It featured Hancock Park girls of high lineage and Jewish girls from Shtetlville West. I saw the wish-named Joan reborn in dozens of Semitic incarnations. I stalked Donna Weiss around Beverly and Gardner. I saw her go to synagogue shindigs and Gilmore Park. She was blondish and curvy. Her features were too big for her face. She wore a demure bikini poolside. Her tan deepened through the summer of 1961. The Berlin Wall fracas almost took the world down. I craved the easy out of nuke devastation. I loved Donna, Cathy, Kay and many window faces seen. I yearned for mental monogamy. It drove me batshit. I wanted one image captured for endless consolation and sex.

There were *too* many girls and women. Hancock Park was ultra-swank and a hotbed of sex within view and reach.

Cathy Montgomery was pure Hancock Park. Kay Olmsted was fringe Hancock Park. The tall brunette. The short blonde with the hurricane-hurled hazel eyes. Villager shirt-dresses for Cathy. A black beret for preppy beatnik Kay.

I hoarded paper-route money and sent both girls big floral bouquets. I was 14. It was my Summer '62 D-day

Assault. The *D* stood for desperate and delirious. I got blow-off/thank-you notes back.

I became a B&E artiste years later. I snuck inside Cathy's house and Kay's house repeatedly *then*. The notion to enter and prowl hadn't hit me yet. My desperation and delirium had yet to peak.

My teenage life stood in arrears. My acceleration was all internalized. I struggled through junior high and into senior high. I had shifting cliques of loser friends and no friends. I taped pictures of Beethoven over my bed and pondered our genius. He composed his greatest music for his "Immortal Beloved." Her identity remained as mysterious as The Other for me. Beethoven understood my deep loneliness and sorrow. His deafness inspired visionary thoughts unknown to mortal men. *My* deafness was voluntary. Beethoven dug that. I often played the adagio of the Hammerklavier Sonata before I went peeping. Beethoven approved more than condemned the practice. Sometimes he'd scowl at me and shake his finger. He never quite told me to grow up and pull my head out of my ass.

I was deaf to the real world and anything that contradicted my monomaniacal private agenda. The 1960s social scene was pixilated newsprint and no more. Nothing in the real world touched me or fazed me. Jack Kennedy got elected, got laid, got whacked. What, *me* worry? Fuck— that's Joanne Anzer. We'll almost *do* it in the Summer of Love. Now she's on TV. Fuck—that's *her*. She's doing the wah-watusi on the Lloyd Thaxton Hop!!!

The word *More* summarized my private agenda. It was sexual compulsion fueled by a terror of human contact and the forfeit of mental control. I could brood, peep, stalk, think and self-narrate. I could not *act*. I understood that conundrum in the moment. A conceit numbed the power of the revelation and pushed me further into a mystical state. I came to believe that certain women could read my aura and detect my prayerful condition. Fait accompli: those women would find me. Our identical passion would then be unified.

Women—not girls. The *mothers* of the girls. The fantasy women who once went at me so powerfully and roughly.

I peeped a dance party at 2nd and Irving. Cathy Montgomery lived two blocks west. Joanne Anzer lived a block north. The party vibed earthquake epicenter. It was fall '63. I had a vague sense that the Twist was dead. Yes and no—dig those middle-aged stiffs doing it now.

Yes and no. The men were stiffs. The women weren't. The women married the stiffs and regretted it now. Every woman I saw danced better than her male partner. There was more hip movement and less inhibition. There was a sense of gyration as a sexual substitute. They condescended to the silly music less and relinquished themselves to it more. It meant more to them because family duty had fizzled and daddy-o was less than they thought. The dance party was a reprieve from the ennui and repressed tenderness that would lead them to me. I sensed sweetly what career womanizers know cold: female discontent is opportunity.

The party lingered as an image bank. I roamed Hancock Park and saw a few of the women I'd seen dancing. They were decontextualized and still breathlessly deep. I corralled one woman's runaway dog. We talked for a few moments. I was 15. She was 45-ish. She looked like my future married lover Karen.

The lightning-rod concept lingered. No women sought me out and proved it valid. Fall '63 extended. My dad had a severe stroke. I capitalized on his hospital stay, ditched school and ran wild.

I stole *Playboy* magazines, second-line stroke books and nudist-colony photo jobs that showed female pubic hair.

I taped pictures all over the pad and tacked the Playmate of the Month up beside Beethoven. I roamed, peeped, shoplifted and brooded from dusk to dawn. I discovered *The Fugitive* on TV.

The title character was my imagined self as sexual igniter. He was running from a murder charge as trumped-up as mine was real. The show was the epic of shifting and lonely America. Love was always unconsummated. Yearning was continuous and transferred monogamously. Dr. Richard Kimble had moments of stunning truth with women weekly. The real world interdicted his efforts to claim them and create a separate world mutually safe. The guest-star actresses were torturously aware and rooted in complex and frustrated selfhood. They all try to love him. He tries to love them all. It never happens. It all goes away.

I fucking lost it and wept every Tuesday night. Every one of them was uncontestably The Other for an hour alone with me.

My father came home from the hospital. He was needy and frail. It infuriated me. I had to remove the skin pix and relinquish my access to the TV. I considered reviving The Curse and decided against it. He was old. He'd be gone soon. I'd survive for more Tuesdays.

It wasn't the way they looked at Dr. Kimble. It was who they were and the path of their hurt up to him.

3

I woke up. I was naked, she was naked, I didn't know where I was.

We were under bedsheets. She was still asleep. I didn't know *who* she was.

I rubbed my face. It felt like a four-day growth. I was clean-shaven at my last recollection.

You sold blood plasma downtown. You hitchhiked to the beach. You met your pal Randy and started drinking. You argued with some hippies. You stood on the Palisades and fulminated. Your tory worldview appalled them. You stormed off then.

Booze blackout—age 23.

I was a fit 160. The woman weighed three bills easy. I *looooved* voluptuousness. My standards were permissive. These were curves I could not condone.

A memory burst hit me. I still had nine bucks left from the blood bank.

My clothes were on the bedside floor. My glasses and wallet were safe. Two twenties were tucked in the billfold.

The woman snored on. Maybe she paid me for it. That would mark a first.

I got up, got dressed and stealth-walked out of the pad. Stairs led down to a ground-floor landing. I stepped outside. I was on Fell Street in San Francisco.

. . .

She was the fourth. Keeping track was easy then. Susan was
#1. She was 29 to my 20. She needed a roof and fucked me
in the Spirit of Revolution. She caught me jacking off on
uppers the night RFK got shot. She defamed me as a perv,
a bum lay and a fascist. She turned dyke for political reasons and the valid motive of inclination.

I was an especially puerile 20 and malleable in the
extreme. I was months into a run of sobbing fits out of pure
sex hunger/angst. Susan had a '60s-zeitgeist spiel down pat.
I believed all of it when we were stoned and none of it when
we were clean. Susan knew a high school pal of mine and
fucked him just as callously. He was even more pliable than
I was and had an even more roach-ridden apartment. His
cystic acne was worse than mine. I could steal drugs from
stores and rich people's houses. He was afraid to. I boded as
a better doormat/pity fuck.

Susan and I guzzled cough syrup and pills swiped from
medicine chests all over Hancock Park. We talked classical
music shit endlessly. We got bombed and played Emil Gilels
and Sviatoslav Richter. We defamed rock and roll as coun-
terrevolutionary pap. Susan endured Beethovian mood
swings and treated me as her mongoloid kid brother and
dope-thief-on-command. All that tsuris got me four per-
emptory fucks. My zits popped in the throes of my real and
her feigned passion. Susan held the line at fuck #5. My
technique had not improved to her specifications. My social
skills were sub-zero. I was staggeringly uncool and required
deep pore cleansing and dermabrasion. Besides—she'd just
met a groovy chick with a cool pad in the Hollywood Hills.

Charlotte was #2. It was late '69. She was an affluent
Palos Verdes girl on post-college hiatus. My booze-brave
approach charmed her. She bought my great-writer-in-
waiting act for three months and wised up. Her inclination:

postpone sex for marriage to a *real* man. Why I got it: the era mandated pre-marital sex as an experiment. We were next-door neighbors and met on the Wilshire Boulevard bus. I held down temp jobs as I brain-broiled the world's greatest unwritten novel. Charlotte thought I drank too much. I pried open movie-house back doors and glommed us free double features. Charlotte thought that was cool and très '69. Charlotte found me too emotional and sex-crazed. Sex was not all day and all night. Sex was a special occasion. Charlotte came to view me as a *dubious* experiment.

The experiment full-on tanked. Charlotte gave me a withering look and skedaddled. The look has since become familiar. It means, You've lied to me and you're not who you say you are.

Christine was #3. She was a zit freak more than a sex freak. We coupled in early '71 and hooked up periodically. I got in fistfights with her numerous boyfriends. Chris was a poetess and a dermatologist manqué. My acne-assaulted back delivered her delighted. She studied cross sections of the human dermis for hours. She bit my right-middle knuckle down to the bone to scope out the cartilage. I've still got the scar. She popped my pimples and examined the pus under a microscope. My first three women treated me as a lab-rat lover.

I stole a pint of vodka and hopped a bus, Frisco back to L.A. I lived in Robert Burns Park that summer. It was Hancock Park–adjacent. The girls I loved and stalked were off in grad school or married to stiffs. They had fulfilled the dashed promise of their mothers at that dance party. Money and safety were horrible temptations. They should have waited for me. I knew I'd sort my shit out at some point in the future.

The '60s sizzled all around me. I remained nonplussed.

My shit solidified and fossilized. I was well into a *looooooong* tailspin.

My dad died in '65. I got kicked out of high school and psych-discharged from three months in the army. I held down minimum-wage jobs and flopped in dive hotels and parks. I smoked weed and scored uppers from dubious physicians. I shoplifted and full-time fantasized. I kept a bust of Beethoven stashed in a bush at Burns Park. I did lightweight jolts in the L.A. County jail system. I was too thin and was developing a chronic cough.

Booze and dope regulated my fantasy life. The theme had only intensified. I remained consumed by women. It was pushing me toward insanity and death.

Tenderness in no way marked my short liaisons. I grasped with suffocating force and trawled for the next image with real women present. I couldn't let go of the hurt or stop telling myself stories. I couldn't stop looking at women and beseeching them to smash my stories and talk back to me.

The only love I knew was pornography self-created. The only lovers I desired radiated a distrust of men that would always exclude me. I succumbed to fantasies of Jean Hilliker and had her for a few dope-depraved seconds. *Evil boy, piety lost, unredeemable searcher.*

The American '60s: even extreme self-indulgence carried limits.

Booze and downers fueled my great-writer fantasies. I read crime books and historical tomes in public libraries. Amphetamines gave me SEX. Dexedrine, Biphetamine, Desoxyn. A gonad-goosing triad. Dick-depleting substances. Eroticizing and *not* counterproductive. *There were no women. They were all in my head.*

The Hancock Park girls. Their mothers. Guest-star actresses on *The Fugitive.* Women glimpsed on my obsessive window peeps.

The fantasies were raw and loving. I holed up in dive pads, gas-station men's rooms and dark public parks. I saw faces, faces and faces. I saw Her, She, Them. There can only be One. The cavalcade of faces must lead to one woman revealed.

I masturbated myself bloody. I brain-screened faces for stern beauty and probity. The dope drizzled out of my system. I drank myself comatose and woke up in random shrubbery and jails. I never questioned the validity of my mission. I never questioned my sanity or the religiousness of my quest. I did not subscribe to the notion of the American 1960s as the *sine qua non* of all behaviors in extremis. I was tracing the arc of The Hilliker Curse. I wanted One Woman or All Women to be Her. The horribly looming price of insanity or death in no way deterred me.

The fuzz started cracking down on dope-script docs. I was big, short-haired and some weird bookish/fierce-looking hybrid. I vibed rookie cop/faux hippie. Nobody would sell me dope.

I roamed around Hancock Park and peeped windows. I got the urge to prowl around *inside*.

Peggy's house, Kay's house, Cathy's house. Missy's house, Julie's house, Joanne's house.

Beautiful Hancock Park houses. *They* lived there. I could smell their secrets and touch their things.

The burglary show ran through the mid to late '60s. It was its own separate blur. There might have been 20 performances. Time disintegrated during the actual process. It weighs big in retrospect. It was a minute proportion of my active watcher's life.

Hancock Park. All those houses. B&E was easy then.

Unanswered phones meant empty dwellings. Pet-access doors were made for me. Push back the rubber flap and trip the inside latch. Genetic determinism. It's why you've got long arms.

Window screens were loosely attached to bent nails. The panes were often pushed up. The first-floor sills were within my reach. I had memorized those details on furtive walk-bys. It was a learning process. I didn't know it until my first break-in.

The idea was to touch Their lives and Them once removed. Don't soil the premises. Don't ransack and leave signs. *You love Them.* You know this is wrong. Don't announce your violation.

Then you can do it again and again. Then you can perpetuate your wrongdoing. This will cosmetically justify your affection.

I succeeded at this pursuit. I did it and never got caught. I had the phone numbers, I knew the neighborhood, I was innocuous on the 10:00 p.m. streets. My backup job was to steal. I filched small bills from purses and small quantities of pills from medicine chests. I raided refrigerators and ate small quantities of food. I poured short shots of liquor, decanter to glass—and always avoided spills.

Careful boy, twisted heart, ever self-serving.

A long prelude up to this. Never covetous of wealth nearby. Never envious in my hunger.

I possessed night vision. I carried a flashlight for the detail work and kept the beam low. The dark was comforting. Unlit rooms console me now. Muted colors thrilled me then. The fabrics were stimulating. Brocade wallpaper and chenille. Things They had touched.

Objects tossed haphazardly. Napkins left behind. A tennis racket propped up with three umbrellas.

Their interiors. An explicit view to complement my all-internal love. Lush sets for fantasies.

Their bedrooms frightened me. Scents came on stronger as colors went too bright. I lay on Their beds and jumped up, that much more afraid. I ran my nose over Their pillows. I touched Their clothes and smelled new things and got the flash of Their everydays.

The rush always made me dizzy. The light-headedness felt like a rewiring I might not survive. I stole sets of lingerie. I pulled hairs out of brushes and held them to my cheek.

The '60s coddled and camouflaged me. I eschewed hippie regalia. My booze stunts got me county-jail time. My craven housebreakings and epic jack-off stints did not. Dope dried up for me. A chance meeting tapped me into an endless legal source.

A hippie guy told me about Benzedrex inhalers.

Cotton wads soaked in an amphetamine-based solution. A nasal decongestant encased in plastic tubes. *Toxic cotton that you swallowed.* An ever-tapable source of jack-off sex— until it destroys your health or kills you.

A stealable drug sold over the counter. A seven-year search engine in my quest for Her.

I swallowed inhaler wads and brain-screened faces. I held down sporadic employment. I got a job at the KCOP-TV mailroom. I stole cash sent in through the mail, banged up the company van and got sacked. I passed out handbills for a Serbo-Croatian psychic. I got a job at an all-night porno bookstore. I raided stacks of beaver-photo books for pictures that might be Her. I stole beaver books and plundered them on my inhaler trips. I tapped the till and got fired for my thefts.

None of the pictures were Her. There was no Her, no She, no The Other. I did not know it *then*. I could not stop looking *then*. I was unstoppable unto the death.

I developed a tolerance for the wads. It took eight to twelve to get me sufficiently high. I saw women's faces and heard taunting voices in my head. They accused me of inflicting The Curse and killing my mother. The shit fucked with my lungs. I got pneumonia twice. Two-week jolts at County General cured me and taught me nothing. I walked out the door and stole more inhalers. I resumed my search for Her again.

I consumed cotton wads in extreme quantity and prowled the streets that had enticed me since childhood. I knew all of the houses, many of the windows and the precise location of prior-seen faces. New windows alerted me to new women. I saw familiar faces—older now, and oddly grave. I retreated to dump hotel rooms and parks and got alone with Them in the dark. The voices in my head got worse. I veered very close to psychosis. I stuffed cotton in my ears and heard the voices that much louder.

I bolted my enclosed settings and walked long distances to deflect the sound. I twitched, lurched and betrayed my mental state. People shied away from me. Women stared briefly and averted their eyes. I always tried to note their faces without scaring them. I know that I always failed at this.

I developed a lung abscess. A giant pus ball ate up my left pleura. I stumbled into a hospital. A month of intravenous antibiotics and daily back pounding killed the fucking thing.

The seven-year search.

For Her, She, The Other.

I survived. God has always had a job for me. I'm the guy who lives to tell you the story.

I met a woman in '73. We ran into each other at a coin Laundromat. I was tailspinning as she was living upright. She was unaccountably kind to me.

Her name was Marcia Sidwell. She was a year younger

than I and worked as a registered nurse. She wore glasses and had reddish blond hair.

We had three conversations at one-week intervals. Marcia initiated the first. She was properly friendly and never flirtatious. I knew that she had surmised my outdoor lifestyle and that she did not judge me unduly. I dredged up a semblance of decorum in an effort to sustain her acquaintance.

Marcia spoke more than I did. We discussed Watergate. Marcia thought my disdain for rock and roll was reflexive and peculiar. She had a somewhat dubious boyfriend. She was vexed by the general male reaction to her big breasts and commended me for not staring. She was not being coy or provocative. I never mentioned my red-haired nurse mother and her 15-year-old death. Marcia had startlingly bright blue eyes. I showed her my grimy Beethoven bust. She touched my arm for a second.

I showed up for a fourth chat. Marcia washed her clothes at the same time every week. I assumed that she'd pull up in her Volkswagen.

She didn't show that day. I waited every day for a month. Marcia never showed up again.

It devastated me. I figured I'd said or done something wrong or betrayed my acute dissolution. My self-absorbed/guilty-boy logic was entirely specious. Marcia found a Laundromat closer to home or opted for some other convenience. Our acquaintanceship meant the world to me and not much to her.

She told me who she was and treated me justly. I wish I could have done something stunningly bold in return.

February '58—the San Gabriel Valley as the Third World–cum–Appalachia. Jean Hilliker and I land in the hellhole hub.

Our house was moldy and confining. Pervasive mildew made me retch and sneeze. Our pachuco-redneck neighbors made my pious soul quake and my baby-pervert skin crawl.

Jean Hilliker was boozing more. She always reeked of rotgut bourbon. She got me that loser dog for my birthday. I knew it came with a price.

She sat me down on the couch. She was half-gassed. She laid out a line of shit pertaining to my rite of passage. *You're a young man now. You're old enough to choose. Would you rather live with your dad or with me?*

I said, My dad.

She hit me.

I fell off the couch and gouged my head on a glass coffee table. Blood burst out of the cut. I called her a drunk and a whore. She knelt down and hit me again. A shutter stop blinked for her. She covered her mouth and pulled away from it all.

Blood trickled into my mouth. I recalled the book, I issued The Curse, I summoned her dead. She was murdered three months later. She died at the apex of my hatred and equally burning lust.

Her crime was passionate and thus forgivable. She inflicted her own damage and repented in true haste. My punishment was callous and premeditated. I parceled my rage and mystically summoned a killer. We are as one in our hunger and rectitude. I owe her for every true thing that I am. I must remove The Curse I have placed on her and on myself. I must revoke her status as The Other.

4

Home again.

I looped back to L.A. in '06. I'd spent 25 years in points north and east and plowed a return course. Two divorces and a crack-up were part of it. My survival sense played in. The real-life Joan dumped me in San Francisco. A married woman I'd met for two seconds lived in L.A. Joan and I had wanted a daughter. The married woman had two daughters. That ghost of a chance pushed me the rest of the way home.

The film version of *The Black Dahlia* was out. It was a critical and box-office dud and a paperback smasheroo. My publisher scheduled a reading at Skylight Books in East Hollywood.

I looked good and felt good and tingled with I'm Back! resurgence. Spirits were nudging me. I missed Joan and my second ex-wife, Helen. I had seen the married woman the night before. Our rapport mutualized. We discussed daughterhood as reality and unfulfilled longing. I pulled the Let's-have-lunch ploy. I doubted that she'd call me. Marcia Sidwell was on my mind in a big way. Thirty-odd years and three dialogues. Marcia *owned* a big and separate part of me.

I'd made stabs at finding her and always came up short. I spent dough on private eyes and deployed my cop pals. I wanted to see her and say thank you. I wanted to do something costly and *large*. Maybe she had a sick kid who needed my spare kidney. Two seconds with those bright blue eyes would tear my heart up.

Skylight was packed. I counted 200 people. A full third were female. A bookstore guy introduced me. My fans went nuts. I noticed a luminous redhead about 50. The guy beside her radiated stooge boyfriend.

I walked to the lectern. I thought, Fuck it, let's try.

I said, "Stop me now. It's going to my head. I need a strong woman to tame me with her love and walk all over me in high black boots."

My fans dug it. A few women whistled. I read from my book, took questions and repeated the line four times. *Get it? I'm scrounging affection.*

It was a knockout performance by my own exalted standards. I signed books for the folks afterward. The redhead waltzed the boyfriend by and showed me her boots. I groaned and clutched the lectern. Seven women slipped me their phone numbers.

I called three of them. We had dinner dates on consecutive evenings. I told them I was between obsessions and needed an intimate friend. *Am I being too abrupt or in any way offensive?*

All three said no and evinced delight. Instant intimacy evolved. The anticipation and hope were softer and weightier than the acts.

I gave another reading the following week. I was played out and boffo regardless. The married woman hadn't called me. I brooded on her incessantly. I stretched out on my bed and talked to her. We discussed daughterhood. Beethoven glowered above us.

The bookstore crowd dispersed. I walked back to my car, dead-ass tired. I noticed a woman at a sidewalk café.

She was the right age. She had similar coloring and identical deportment.

I caught her eye and said, "Marcia?"

She blinked and said, "No."

The married woman called me the next day.

PART II

THEM

5

I want to hold your hand.

That was the concluding shtick. You sat through the drunk-and-dopealogs and laced up for the Lord's Prayer. Ninety minutes of confession for twenty seconds of skin. I had to reconstruct my life. That felt like drudge work. The dykey redhead felt like momentary payoff.

My first AA meeting. Monday, August 1, 1977.

I was 29. I had survived the seven-year run of inhaler wads and psychoses. I quit booze, weed and pharmaceutical uppers. My new regime was abstinence. It boded horrific. I quit shoplifting and breaking into houses. I had not had a spiritual awakening. Brain-screening women's faces had almost killed me. My compulsive appetite had now hung a 360. The straight and narrow beckoned. A ruthless self-interest defined my apostasy. I wanted women. I wanted to write novels. Sobriety meant efficacy. I couldn't advance my agenda in my current raggedy-ass state.

The meeting dragged on. Most people smoked. The fumes tickled my healing lung tissue. A guy called the red-head "Leslie." She looked like a low-rent Marcia Sidwell. The hand-holding ended. Leslie never glanced at me. You came that far for *this*?

. . .

Things weren't *that* bad. My chronic cough was cured. I was young and heroically resilient. I had a caddy gig at the Bel-Air Country Club. I had a twenty-dollar-a-week hotel room. The communal bathrooms and shower were down the hall. The in-room sink was a pissoir.

A new Beethoven poster loomed above my bed. I played the Master's soaring psalms on an eight-track contraption and brooded. A late-blooming moral sense kept me from peeping. I *peered* now. I roamed Westwood Village, stared and stopped short of approach. I possessed no notion of a social code. The world was still hazy. The sexual revolution applied to other folks. The permissiveness of the era belonged to the cute and the glib. I was a tenuously reformed pervert, adrift.

My sex urge had almost killed me. It was drug-driven and solitary. It's a still-memorable blur of female faces. I credited God with the save and pondered His mission for me. It came down to write books and find The Other. That was 33 years ago. The faces swirl inside me decades later. The women remain as images seeking a narrative thread. They did not know who I was then and do not know who I am now. Real women have joined them. Real experience and active discourse have in no way dissolved the blur. My lustful heart has expanded to keep them all in.

I almost died. I attributed my malady to The Curse. It was divine punishment and collateral damage to the death I'd caused. I spun shameful fantasies of Jean Hilliker and paid a near-fatal price for that Curse-derived transgression. My mother was 19 years dead. I carried no love for her and ignored my debt to her. I feared her power and nullified it by banishing her from my mind.

My hotel room was narrow and underfurnished. I kept it spotlessly clean. I rarely turned the lights on. I played Beethoven and his lesser acolytes and brain-talked to women, dead sober.

Faces whooshed by from my childhood. The Hancock Park girls were there. The wish-named Joan appeared often. I mentally aged her to 38 years and reveled in her power as a prophet. The real Joan turned 12 that year.

It was mental brushwork. I was creating a visual palette with a newly urgent sound track. I was desperate to write stories and touch women for real. I heard women's confessions in AA. I weighed their depictions of gender bias and sexual trauma, unfettered by notions of male supremacy. I conversed with them in the dark. I was consoler, interlocutor, friend. Seduction was mutually proffered in deep empathy. Sex expressed our lives of thwarted hunger up to that first kiss.

The fantasy was endlessly repetitive and easily transferred. I went from face to face, in search of probity and sex transcendent. I embraced woman images discerningly and abandoned them callously. Sobriety enhanced my fantasist's prowess and fucked with my powers of suppression. I felt voodooized. It was a crybaby crisis and punch-the-wall fury fit. It drove me to the point of action.

With the knowledge that women would not read my mind and thus detect my prayerful condition.

With the knowledge that my moral intent vibed pure lust.

With the knowledge that women did not view me as a savior and were, in fact, terrified of me.

I lurked in bookstores near the UCLA campus. I read women's faces for character and a sense of humor that might mark them as susceptible to my charm. I miscalculated here. I possessed no charm and oozed nervous tension. My pickup lines all pertained to books and were all levied on women who appeared to be self-assured and brainy. They had survived the stringent first cut: no heavy makeup, no nail polish, no sexy chick affect or rock-and-roll trappings. I was seeking a blend of wholesomeness and hot passion. I was looking for a fellow autodidact oblivious to trend.

The first run of women rejected me fast. I betrayed myself instantly. Conversation sandbagged me. My mouth twitched, my beady eyes burned, my jerky body set off alarms. My glasses slid down my nose. I displayed stubby teeth caused by losing fistfights and poor dental care. I was an SOS call. Women knew it immediately. The brushoffs convinced me to readjust my criteria and up the spiritual ante.

Only lonely and haunted women would grok my gravity. They were sister misfits attuned to my wavelength. Only *they* grooved internal discourse and sex as sanctified flame. Their soiled souls were socked in sync with yours truly.

My rationale was *that* convoluted. My love seeking was that mystical and predatory. I threw myself at a second run of record-store women. They possessed less than stellar world-standard looks and were stunningly un-svelte. I dug them and wanted them anyway.

They *all* blew me off. My opening salvos *all* pertained to Beethoven. They were *all* perusing classical music LPs. I flopped again. Their alarms scree-screed. A Beethovian principle was at work here. Beethoven was the only artist in history to rival the unknown and unpublished Ellroy. He was a fellow brooder, nose picker and ball scratcher. He yearned for women in silent solitude. His soul volume ran at my shrieking decibel. You and me, kid:

Her, She, The Immortal Beloved/The Other. Conjunction, communion, consecration and the completion of the whole. The human race advanced and all souls salved as two souls unite. The sacred merging of art and sex to touch God.

Those women could not have read my heart. My heart would have horrified them.

I want to crawl up inside you and offer you the same comfort. Cup my ears. I'll do the same for you. The scream of the world is unbearable and only we know what it means.

I put that out to total strangers. My botched repartee was the scream. It was the high-note dissonance in Beethoven's late quartets. I remained that obsessed in a dead-sober state. There was no hint of abatement and no sign of release.

Sobriety kicked in. That death scare kept me focused. The dutiful part of my nature got buttressed all day every day. AA offered me absolutism and a compatible latitude in my faith. Half of my sober comrades were women. I studied them and tore through unrequited crushes at great speed. They joined me in the dark. I reconstructed the words they spoke in meetings and altered the meaning of their lives to spotlight their fictive love for me.

It was all about recognition. The dialogue was encapsulated 50/50. We shared the truth of our lives on an equal basis and kissed. We stepped back from the brink of precipitous passion, pledged monogamy and made love. I masturbated then. That part of my sojourn ended abruptly. *Whew*—now we can talk about what it all *means*.

Soft-focus pix scrolled along with the pillow talk. Women never seen naked appeared in the buff beside me. Melinda D. folds a breast back to burrow closer in. I touch the acne scars on Pat J.'s neck to tell her it's okay. She shakes her head, removes my hand and goes, Hush now. Moonlight beams through my dive hotel window. Laurie B.'s got tears in her eyes. I'm smiling because she just said, I love you. She laughs and tugs at my grotesque little teeth.

It was like that. It was over 30 years ago—and I cannot let go of one moment of it.

Deep talk, lovemaking, deep talk. Sweat and nicotine breath back when classy women still smoked. The pledge of a shared future. The common cause of *Us*. The analysis of our shared pasts to vouchsafe a utopian future. Their real stories and my reinterpretation. My disingenuous omission of the dead woman hovering. My savior shtick and their capitulation to it. Their vow to assuage my big hurt. My vow to kick the shit out of every male being who had ever done them wrong. Our certainty that we would never cheat and that it would always be this *gooooooooood*.

Deep talk, lovemaking, deep talk. On a transferably monogamous nightly basis, with any woman who might be Her.

Crazy boy, all mental tricks, artist manqué.

This fever consumed a full year. Shifting soul currents defined it. My physical anguish increased. The pillow-talk patterns swerved. The real world called again. I had to have Her *now*. I remained immobilized. I listened to the fantasy Her less and talked to the fantasy Her more. I lived in the stimulus of Her and raged to rewrite Her life to my own specifications. Passion circumscribed by the flow of perception. Life stories revised to suit my narrative needs and to sate my huge and defective ego. A training course for a ruthlessly ambitious young man, guilt-racked and devoutly religious at his core.

"I will take Fate by the throat." Beethoven's shout at his advancing deafness. The Master's chaste solitude and my retrospective conviction: art is this dialogue with untouchable spirits—and what you grasp for you can write.

My stimulation index exploded. Hookers invaded the Sunset Strip en masse.

It was '78. The Hillside Strangler panic had raged and subsided. No more Hollywood abductions. The fucker had vanished. My prayers for the fucker's capture went unanswered. I observed the upshot.

Prostitutes swarmed Sunset for solid miles. Some wore skeevy whore threads and garish makeup. Most dressed like normal women. They seemed to represent a new love-for-sale lifestyle. If they were selling, I was buying.

I knew some cops from AA. They gave me the lowdown. The women were "weekenders." Some were "actresses" looking to score extra bread. Most were office workers and schoolteachers, branching out from Bakersfield and San Berdoo. They jungled up in motels and found safety in numbers. Sure, they looked normal. But—no normal chick peddles her ass for gelt.

The appearance of normalcy jazzed me. I sensed individual stories shaped by specious social codes. One cop cited cocaine. One cop cited rogue feminism. One cop cited greed. Shake yo booty—the times, they are a-changin'.

The women seemed *real*. I borrowed cars, cruised the Strip and scanned faces. I read their eyes, sensed what brought them there and what would convince them to stop. The women clogged the sidewalk from 8:00 p.m. on. I made dozens of recon circuits. I scanned for wholesome faces and evidence of cracking facades. I detoured then. I drove Sunset east to Bunker Hill. I staked out the Dorothy Chandler Pavilion.

Symphony concerts ended around 10:00 p.m. Women with violins and cellos scooted out rear exits. I was a tongue-tied stage-door Johnny. Most of the women met their husbands and boyfriends. They wore tight black orchestra gowns with cinched waists and plunging necklines. They looked anxious to shuck their work duds, belt a few and talk music. Single women walked out, lugging heavy instruments. I offered to help several of them. They all said no.

Back to the Strip. Back to reading faces. Back to the honing of my Let's-buy-sex aesthetic.

I liked the women older than I. I thought they might be more grateful for my biz and be more responsive. I liked the women with glasses. I liked the women with creased brows that said, Hooking might not be kosher.

It took two dozen drive-bys and blow-offs with the L.A. Philharmonic. I saved up some coin, borrowed a car and pounced.

It was midweek. It was cold. Rainstorms had blown through L.A. The Strip was packed. The women wore puffy windbreakers and buckskin dusters. I noticed a solitary pro upside Hollywood High. She wore granny glasses. She was rangy and fair-haired. She wore a slinky skirt under a toggle coat. It was affectless and *sweet*. It was a geek's idea of sexy attire. She was seven or eight years older than I and appeared to be nervous. I extrapolated her life story instantly—and to my mind, adroitly. College prof on the skids. A history of weak men. A disengaged notion of prostitution as a lab experiment.

I pulled to the curb. She walked to the car and leaned in the passenger-side window. I said, Hello. She asked me if I was a cop. I asked her why she thought that.

She mentioned my short hair. I justified the close-cropped style and told her I worked at a golf course. She said, You just want to be different.

The perception delighted me. She had a flat, midwestern voice. She said it was twenty for French and thirty for half-and-half. I said I had a C-note and just wanted a decent stretch of her time. She looked at her watch and asked me if I wanted something special. I said, Just some time with you. Her look said, Oh—you're one of those.

She directed me to a motel, four blocks away on La Brea. The room was twice the size of my room and still small. She locked us in and pointed to the dresser. I laid five twenties down.

The room was warm. My legs fluttered and dripped sweat. She took off her coat and tossed it on a chair. She had soft arms for such a slender woman. An image hit me: Vera Miles as a cocktail-lounge artiste in *The Fugitive*. She scooped the money into her purse. I said, We don't have to do it. She said, I'll kick you out if you cry.

I leaned against the wall and shut my eyes. She told me not to make it into such a big deal. I opened my eyes. She unbuttoned her blouse. I asked her where she was from. She said, Fullerton.

An Orange County college town. My theory validated. I started to say some—

She unhooked her bra. I saw her breasts and smiled. She said, That's better. I took her right hand and kissed her arm above the elbow. She jiggled my hand and said, Lighten up. Okay?

Deep breaths tamped my rev down. She kicked off her shoes and kept her socks on. She pulled off her skirt and underwear and stood there.

She said, Okay?

The room tumbled.

It was rushed after that. It was rushed because she wanted it to be over and I didn't want to embarrass or displease her.

She didn't want to talk.

She dodged my questions.

She wouldn't let me hold her.

I don't know how long it all lasted. It felt like the world revealed.

So I did it repeatedly—with weirdo intuition and horny pastor's kid intent.

The count was high, overpayment kept me broke, my

criteria was unique. The swirl of available faces kept on coming.

Borrowed pervmobiles got me to the Strip and home again, laid and unsated. Runs by the Dorothy Chandler Pavilion counterbalanced and ratched up my rev. I aroused suspicion at both locations. The Hillside Strangler was a fresh local horror. I cruised the same turf. Why are you offering me extra money? No, I don't need you to carry my cello.

I understood the distinctions between the two professions and treated both sets of women the same. I looked for a cultural component in the hookers and a brusque wantonness in the string players. I got action from the former and zilch from the latter. My extreme acuity was delusional and acutely self-serving. I read faces for signs of the worthiness of love and demanded reciprocated love instantly. It was all crude male barter—money and mock-impromptu favors. I came in with prepared text and crumbled at the first sign of improvisation. Prostitutes did not want to hear my rationale for buying their body. Violinists did not want my loser ass— they wanted a straight Sviatoslav Richter. Both groups saw me as a zealot with a smoke-screened agenda.

The prostitutes put faith in the banality of sex and trusted fuck me–pay me men on that basis. I could not accept the implied dictum. The musicians viewed sex as an intergrated aspect of their lives in search of refinement. That idea was just as restrictive. The proper answer is sex is *everything*—so show me the faces and I'll write the story.

My agenda was women as muse. I ran the entire gender through an obstacle course. The few and the proud cleared the last hurdle. Selected prostitutes survived a run of drive-by sightings and were deemed fit to be with me once and reside in me forever. The musicians survived chastely. I never lugged their instruments. I got a few smiles that sent me through to next week.

The Strip to the Dorothy Chandler Pavilion and back again. My selection process. A C-note offered for this: Can we get naked and talk a bit?

I logged three refusals. It worked four times. It depressurized the girls. It got me softness, taxed sighs and conversation. The thrill was the undressing and the staged tableaux. I heard stories of bad dads, cheating hubbies at Camp Pendleton and freaky Uncle Harold. I snagged my prey later in the evening. They were tired and pleased to find a low-exertion john. I studied them as I pressed close. They were saving bread to open a boutique. They needed coin for a retarded kid's schooling. They were post-sex or above sex. They were feminist pragmatists hopped up on some paperback doctrine. They pooh-poohed the idea of sex as the biggest deal on earth. They gave me a pinpoint moment of their lives and were grateful that I granted it importance.

I learned to chat a little. I learned a few sensual tricks. Do this or this—you might have a girlfriend one day. You're a sweet guy, get your teeth fixed, don't *stare* so much. What's going on in that weird head?

I told two of them. I said I wanted to write novels. I loved crime fiction and classical music. My brain was overamped. I walked to my golf-course job and dawdled to look at women. Drama was a man meets a woman. Violent events intercede. The man and woman are swept away by catastrophic corruption. They confront a series of morally unhinged people who need to be interdicted and quashed. The man and woman cannot run from this malfeasance.

The moral point of struggle is to overcome it and change. It scares me to think that real love/sex flatlines and dies over time. I want real love and will find real love and will not let it numb my imagination. You're drawing me little pictures. We're here to tell each other special things. I don't care if you're just trying to be nice and I'm paying you for it. Women take me someplace thunderous and hang me out to dry. I want to write from that romantic perspective. You rewire my heart and show me how shit works. You talk to me and listen to me. It's the world in a pop-up book I can understand.

Yeah, but I'm naked.

Well, I'm naked, too.

You're not going to ask for something creepy.

No, I'm not.

I had that conversation four times. Stunned looks and soft looks followed. The last woman and I talked until 2:00 a.m. She was a ranch worker from Kern County. She kept her hands laced behind her head. I kissed her underarms at pause points in my monologues. It seemed to delight her. We didn't have sex. We faded out and slept together. She leaned into me and held my left wrist.

The mojo built that way. The faces cohered over my watcher's lifetime. Faux pillow talk and real talk at hot-sheet motels. Spirits revised at the expense of their probable truth.

The story sprang from a grab at the women I couldn't have and loomed as big as their mythic construction. I was easily transmogrified to a music-mad private eye. He came from the poor edge of Hancock Park. He was recently sober. His mother hadn't been murdered. He didn't stalk rich girls and rip off their pads. I deleted the pathos of near-fatal masturbation. This fucker had more dignity.

The woman played the cello. She looked like the wish-named Joan. The real Joan turned 14 that year.

The fictive woman's body language derived from hookers in assessment. Her contours were those of AA women I had brain-screened in the nude. Her temperament was that of Jean Hilliker. Her gaze prophesied the real Joan and my married lover Karen. There were brief glimpses of the conjuress Erika.

The plot was a crime-book patchwork. The locale was a rigorously de-slime-zoned L.A. There was no El Monte. I didn't have the balls. There was no Hancock Park, with all its attendant perversion.

I avoided Hancock Park. I stayed north of 1st Street, south of 6th Street, west of Highland and east of Western. I zoomed by that Laundromat once a month to look for Marcia Sidwell. She was never there. They were quick-search missions. I swooped by and got out.

Verboten! Don't do it! You're a new man! Barbed-wire noose, poisoned well, danger ahead!

The houses were still beacons. Remnants of the girls still raged there. I could not let myself go back.

6

Women fall asleep first. Penny taught me that. Lover's insomnia—a primer.

She's right beside you, she's naked, you've already made love. She's insensate. You're wired. You're talking to her. She's oblivious. You didn't pay her to listen. She's not talking back.

Penny's bed was short and narrow. I was long-limbed and love-looped and liked to sprawl. Penny had perfected her sleep-with-men posture. She always rolled away on her side and created a gap. It was symbolic. She reposed within inches. It was somewhere off Planet Earth.

I scooted closer. I let my foot brush her leg. I had reinstigated contact. Then I started talking to her in the dark.

About her, about me, about *Us*. About her law-school studies and my book in progress. I spent occasional weekend nights at her whim. Penny would sleep in. I got up predawn and zoomed to the golf course.

The bed was a minefield. I never slept.

I craved more contact. I ran breathlessly anxious. She never said she loved me. The relationship was tenuous and unpredictable. I lay there and anticipated movement. A knee tucked my way marked confirmation. I clenched my bladder until 5:00 a.m. I fantasy-talked to Penny. I fantasy-talked to other women and felt guilty about it. Turnovers filled me with gratitude. Pull-aways filled me with dread. She's your first sober love and she won't say the words. It's not supposed to be this way. You had it all planned out.

We met in June '79. I was six months off of the whore patrol and five months into my first book. I oozed self-confidence. It was fully justified. I was certifiably hot shit. I rocked with a sense of destiny and exuded a raucous panache. My clergymen ancestors streaked through my soul and anointed me with their calling. They had pulpits. I had my book and AA lecterns. I now had *two* stories to tell.

I told my life story to a captive audience. I became a dazzling public speaker at the get-go. Years of mental rehearsal had prepared me. A conscious resolve shaped my testimony. I turned my sex urge to death's door into comedy. I omitted certain details.

No murdered mother. No bloody coughing fits. The jack-off man and his loony lust—*that's* picaresque.

It got me laughs from the AA folks. The book gave me that life's composite woman with the cello.

My hero meets her in a park I used to sleep in. She's poised on a bench with her Stradivarius. My hero hears strains of Dvořák and goes batshit. I meet Penny in a supermarket checkout line. She's buying her nephew a Hula-hoop.

I got her phone number and called her. I blathered and tried to make a groovy impression. I mentioned classical music in due haste. Penny's reaction was, Fuck that shit—I dig rock and roll.

She was 26 years old and from Brooklyn, New York. She had an East Coast accent and a slight lisp. She was Jewish. That appealed to me. It would force me to atone for prior anti-Semitism. She was a big, knock-kneed woman with auburn hair and brown eyes. She was wary and warm at oddly equal intervals. She'd been through a string of boyfriends in a '70s manner and seemed amused by me. She had a married lover stashed someplace. He was a heavyweight lawyer. *Don't be bummed by this. Don't be so intense. You can be my main squeeze.*

Equivocation, mitigation, compromise at the gate. The suggestion of inimical values. A thorny personality. Better socialized than I. Respectful of my wild-ass path and in no way floored by it. Offering communion on her terms—take it or leave it.

Well . . .

We kissed on our first date. We were in Penny's car. It was a classic mutual lean-in. That part conformed to my script. Then Penny said, No—like this.

I almost ran. The correction racked me. She had a car. I didn't. She would become a lawyer. I might write an unpublished book.

I leaned away, leaned back in and kissed her the right way. We kissed three more times. I understood that kiss #4 might be rejected. I said good night before Penny could.

Date #2 was delirious. I showed up at Penny's pad with flowers. She noticed my erection and rolled her eyes. She wanted to rent bicycles and ride a path at the beach. I hated all antic activities. My reaction showed. Penny mollified me and tried not to act impatient.

I blew my roll on the rentals and a burger lunch. That meant extra work at the golf course. We rode the bikes single file. We couldn't talk. It was existential anguish and a macho-mangled loss of control. I got pulsingly paranoid. I thought I saw Penny checking out a black dude. Danger! Danger! Danger! I detoured to the Dick-Size Diaspora. Penny might be a coal burner! What if she required a hard black yard?

Lunch was torture. My stomach churned, my eyes darted. I orbed to Penny's breasts and Penny's eyes. Was she trawling for dark meat or measuring baskets? She caught my eyeball track. She said, Don't be so intense. I said, Can we go someplace and talk? Penny said, Your place?

It was a first-time afternooner. It felt precipitous. My movies never equaled their coming attractions.

The move-in was synchronous. I kissed per Penny's date #1 instructions. My bed was as too-small as her bed would be. It was over too fast. A shared desire for release pushed us through. I wanted marriage, daughters and a crib in Brentwood. Penny wanted an open-ended blast.

Okay, let's *talk* now. You go first. I'm here to *listen*.

Penny said she couldn't. She lisped those words and shook her head. She had to go home and study tort law.

Her slouchy scope moved me. Her clumsiness ripped me up. She chewed her nails. Her hands were as big as mine. She was both ill at ease and content in her body.

We loomed over people. She was five ten, I was six three. We were similarly awkward and bruised from bumps into fixed objects. Walking entwined was dicey. We kept tripping each other.

Late lessons unfolded. I was 31 and an unschooled zealot. I was covetous, jealous and possessive. I never questioned Penny's honor. I lived in fear of her contentiousness and a streak of emotional absence. It was a fight I had to win. I was irrepressibly vigilant. I was always watching and assessing. I wanted Penny. She possessed significant human value and stood up to me. We were both intransigent and fearful. She was *of* me and therefore worthy of my obsessive attention. We were alternately brutally willful and sadsackish. Her intelligence was diffuse and unimpeded by conceit. My brainpower was didactic and stupefyingly attuned to personal advancement.

Penny lived in the world. She had a family, friends,

acquaintances, colleagues, classmates. Her self-worth was undercut with a loopy irony. My mission was to grant her importance. The Curse carried a debt of formal acknowledgment. She should allot herself more power as a woman and assume potent destiny as her birthright. My assumptions were a lover's perceptive gift *and* the shuck of a controlling maniac.

That's what gets me. *That's* how I misdiagnose female personae. *That's* the twisted core of my love-starved largesse.

I recast Penny in my own image. I superimposed my drive upon her—because I was delivered from self-destructive doom, and the corollary of exalted design sure as shit worked for me. That was my grave disservice, whatever my intent.

Penny was smart, funny, honest, kind and proficient. The dumbfounding truth in retrospect: she was different from me.

And we had a groovy kid-lover time—when I eased up a little bit.

Sex was sweaty and clumsy. Long arms and legs flailed. Nightstands collapsed, bathroom fixtures caved, pictures fell off of walls. Debate was active. Topical chat was frazzled. Penny yelled and sulked more than I did. My game was to apologize and re-seduce. Penny always evinced forgiveness—because I always listened to her and always showed up.

She kept me high-wire tense. She withheld the love talk I craved. My anxiety and desire *sizzzzzzled*. She believed in my self-expressed and unconfirmed talent. She never lied to me. She dumped me, lured me back and put out one-night-only calls that I always jumped at. No marriage, no daughters, no possessive pronouns. Constant heartache and no narrative line.

I stayed in the fight. I fixed on Penny's formative trauma and tried to salve her there. Her trauma was less hyperbolic than mine. She allotted her trauma a sane contemplation and not much more. She was not out to exploit her demons for public renown.

You know, I'm not you. Won't you please lighten up?

No, I will not.

Penny had that married lover. She'd dropped details on occasion. I called him a "Jew cocksucker." Penny kicked me. I boo-hooed and repented. Penny laughed and took me to bed.

I was fighting a two-front war. There's Penny. There's my book and the woman with the cello. Beethoven had engaged in similar combat. There's the "Immortal Beloved." There's comely piano students in the meantime. Embrace me, my darling. Later, babe—I gotta write the Fifth Symphony, and I can't hear you anyway.

The presence of the married guy sanctioned me to prowl. I went at it, full speed.

I re-faced another set of women and melded them into my blur. They were *real* women. I met them, talked to them, courted them and had brief liaisons. My new self-confidence inured me to rejection. I jumped on "Yes," tried again at "Maybe," packed my tent at "No." There were AA women and nude coffee dates at "Hot Tub Fever." It was 1980. Java in the buff was risqué and less than a wolf call. I met women in restaurants and movie-theater lines. I got a lot of phone numbers and developed phone-talk relationships. I waited in the dark for the phone to ring. That's still my nightly MO. The phone rings or doesn't ring now. The phone rang or didn't ring then. Dead air, vibelessness and swinging conversation.

The women were indistinguishable and each and every one unique. They informed me that the world had turned a corner with sex and that it had become less mystical. I replied that I knew this. Experience had demystified me. Experience had not dampened my ardor or altered the goddess-worshiping scope of my quest.

My telephone and dive pad were conduits. I worked at the golf course, wrote my book and waited for the phone to ring. The phone rang intermittently. Women called me back or dug out that note slip with my name and number. There was a good deal of sex and no sex and sex as a topic of discussion. I picked the women discerningly. I wanted women who could talk and interpose questions. The era was self-absorbed. Candor was a facet of the freewheeling lifestyle. Phone calls overlapped. Deep talk ensued. I zoomed to strange addresses to have sex or not have sex or roll around clothed. I took on a confessor role. There was a vampiric edge to it. I wanted the women to be fucked-up, so that they would need me.

The counselor role came easy. I was actively pursuing my life's mission and had empathy to burn. I was happy because I was writing a book and was engulfed by women. They got me out of myself and back into myself and returned me refueled to the woman with the cello. The story proceeded apace with my brooding sessions and phone calls. The fictive me is that breathless first-person detective. He's been morally reawakened and sees the woman with the cello as his payoff. He will be with her tenuously and lose her in the end. He will be alone with her memory and wait for a new grail to seek. He will exist in a solitary and dark-roomed state. My first novel predicted the through-line of my life. I didn't know it then.

Calls came in, calls went out, I got numbers and distributed my number. Penny bombed through my life, unpredictably. She still had that married geek. She sensed my independent action and adopted a "Don't ask" policy.

Always the faces, always the blur, sometimes the faces bodied. I got *de*mystified and *re*mystified at the height of this new swirl. I knew I was looking for one face for one purpose. The phone-call women had validated my skewed propriety. They were good, solid humans. Their faces had played out true. I started Identi-Kit building from their physical pool. I wanted to finish my first book and start a new book quick. It would be set in 1951. I needed a face for the lonely and haunted woman in quintessence. I brain-bopped through my current life and my voyeur's path to date and came up empty. A rainy-night dream gave her to me.

She was tall and strong-featured. Her hair was near red and not blond. She wore crooked-fitting glasses and squinted without them. She came forward in laughter and nearly gasped in retreat. Mark me a prophet and recast my mysticism years later. She was my married lover Karen's identical twin.

I possess prophetic powers. Their composition: extreme single-mindedness, superhuman persistence and the ability to ignore intrusions inflicted by the real world. I believe in invisibility. It is a conscious by-product of my practical Christianity, honed by years spent alone in the dark. Faith magnetizes me. It allows me to adhere to the world as I trek a narrow path through it. I am most moved by what I sense coming and can in no way actually see. I pull stories out of thin air. I know that women I have summoned in dreams and mental snapshots will make their way to me. Divine presence forms the core of my gift. I knew the dream woman would materialize in her fully visualized form. I did not know that she was 17 years old in 1980 or that she was a Greek girl from Bumfuck, Queens. I was a solipsistic and chauvinistic prophet. I did not grant women the gift of con-juring. A 16-year-old girl named Erika lived one borough over from Karen. I did not know that she existed or that she was the sorceress who would ultimately summon me.

I finished my first book and started my second book a month later. I was consumed with a hyper-feverish urge to tell stories. Jean Hilliker had been dead for 21 years and six months. My *re*mystification had *de*mystified The Curse. I was *happy*. I had nullified the red-haired girl from Shitsville, Wisconsin. Now I could trump her. Now I could write her story as fiction and quash The Curse flat.

Heedless boy, how could you know?, fate calls you home late.

My new hero was a womanizing cop. He had predatory instincts and my seeker's rationale. Karen's presaged twin showed up early in the text. Jean Hilliker showed up dead, under a pseudonym. A guy based on my dad killed my mom. The cop meets a lawyer based on Penny. A dipshit kid represents me at age nine. The cop and the lawyer rescue his sanitized ass.

A family ripped asunder and a family reborn. Isn't that sweet?

It worked dramatically. It further entombed Jean Hilliker and postponed the rush of The Curse.

I dedicated the second book to Penny. She swooned over the manuscript and declined to sleep with me that night.

Both books were sold to a publisher. The combined advance was chump change. I decided to move to New York. L.A. felt old and constricting. Fewer phone calls were coming in. I sensed that the women had found real lovers. My time in the dark felt reductive. I was unstoppable and none of Them was Her, She or The Other. New York would provide me with a whole new swirl.

I made some good-bye calls. None of the women called

me back. Penny and I had a last nooner. The hookers had vaporized off the Sunset Strip. The Hancock Park houses looked the same. I checked for Marcia Sidwell in half a dozen phone books and didn't find her. The real Joan turned 16 that year. Dream-woman Karen turned 18. Erika the sorceress turned 17.

I looked Penny up in '07. She was 54. She was married, had a teenaged son and lawyered for the state AG. She'd read most of my books. Our first phone chat was a catch-up.

She asked me how many ex-wives and daughters I had. I said, Two and none. She asked me if I still sat in the dark by the phone. I confirmed it. She said, You'll always do that.

7

Paperback writer.

My first book was called *Brown's Requiem*. It hit the stands in September '81. It sold scant copies. There was no author photo and no woman with a cello represented. The cover sucked Airedale dicks. Fuck—a man with a gun and a golf course.

I found a basement pad in Westchester County. I got a caddy job at Wykagyl Country Club. The Big Apple was a train hop south. I blew my book cash on Hancock Park threads gauged for cold weather. I dressed up for jaunts to Manhattan. I knew She'd be there.

My book agent quit the biz and offered me some referrals. My third manuscript was white-hot and ready to unload. It was a sex-fiend cop versus sex-fiend killer turkey. Two male agents urged extensive rewrites. A female agent *looooved* the book and thought I was cute. New York, the go-go '80s, a slinky woman of pedigree. She had hard brown eyes. She cleaned her glasses on her blouse tails and soft-focused her heart. We had dinner and a nightcap at her place. She played me a new record—the Pointer Sisters, with "Slow Hand."

It was sexy shit. I believed the message of *make love now.*

The bedroom faced north. The Empire State Building filled the window. The spire was lit up red, white and green.

The woman and I undressed. This ardent arriviste had arrived.

The basement was my all-time darkest brood den. The lady upstairs was a conductor's widow. Music kept lilting through my vents. She went too heavy on the Mozart and too light on the Liszt. I didn't care. My publisher rejected my third novel. They found the sex-fiend cop and his feminist-poet girlfriend hard to believe. They were right. I wrote the book in a Let's-ditch-L.A.-and-find-HER-in-New-York fugue state. My quasi-girlfriend agent sent the book to 17 other publishers. They all said nyet. My quasi-agent girlfriend dropped me as a client and pink-slipped me as a quasi-boyfriend. I owed her $150 for Xerox fees. I paid her off with extra golf-course bread.

A male agent coerced me into a rewrite. I went at it, reluctantly. Winter hit. Caddy season ended. I worked dish-washer and stockroom gigs and lived ultra-cheap. Manhattan magnetized me. The faces popped out of dense sidewalk traffic. The women were overcoated, hatted and scarved. I couldn't see enough skin to read auras. Cold air and breath condensation. Voyeur prowls deterred.

I habituated coffee bars and got numbers. I got callbacks at a low percentage of my L.A. rate. I lived in the "burbs." That was déclassé. You wrote a book. So? You schlep bags at a golf club. Stockbrokers are more my meat.

The burbs were sexile. I kept hearing that. I lacked lifestyle loot. I kept hearing *that*. Publishing parties got me *some* clout and indoor access. I saw the first Her at a Murray Hill bash.

She was a big preppy woman. She ran six feet and probably outweighed me. Tartan skirt, winter boots, burning eyes and freckles. She was THE OTHER, assuredly.

I walked to the can, combed my hair and adjusted my

necktie. I popped back to the party. She vanished—auf Wiedersehen.

I prowled the surrounding blocks and didn't see her. I went back to the bash and interrogated the guests. I came on too persistent. The host suggested that I leave. I flipped his necktie into his face and skedaddled.

The night was cold. The moon was full. I walked up Fifth Avenue, baying. Passersby swerved around me. Dogs bayed back from swank apartments. I cut east on 43rd Street and hotfooted it toward Grand Central. I saw a woman hailing a cab just west of Madison. The Brooks Brothers' windows golden-glowed her. She was blond. Her overcoat was mud-spattered. She wore red leather gloves. She was shivering. Her face was goose-bumped, her hair was askew, she'd chewed off her lipstick. Her nose was too big. Her chin was too strong. She was THE OTHER, uncontestably.

I fast-walked toward her. An eastbound cab pulled by me. The woman opened the door and got in the backseat. I sprinted, slid on my feet and hit the rear bumper. The woman looked around and saw me. I winced. My knees got ratched from the collision. I smiled. It spooked the woman. She looked away. The cab turned northbound and brodied on hard snow.

Easy come, easy go. It was cold. My knees hurt. I could relive the heavy heartache back at my pad. Douse the lights and spin the Chopin nocturnes. Baby, we were *close*. *It should have been.*

I limped to Grand Central. The waiting room was crowded and overheated. I bought my ticket and walked onto the train. I saw the woman. She was THE OTHER, incontrovertibly.

She was tall, sandy-haired and ten years older than I. She had grail-grabbing gray eyes and a gaunt and sweet face.

She was carrying a cumbersome portfolio. I helped her hoist it to the rack above the seats. She thanked me. We sat down together and talked.

Her name was Marge. She was a commercial artist. She'd been showing work samples at ad agencies all day. I asked her how it went. She said, Bad. She was in a dry spell. She inquired about my employment. I told her I'd written two published books and worked at a country club. *Your family? I don't have one.*

She smelled like wet wool and dissipating eau de bath. She sat on my right. Her damp hair brushed my jacket. She asked me where I detrained. I said, Bronxville. I said, Your destination? She said, Tarrytown.

The train chugged through northern Manhattan and the Bronx. Milk-run stops slowed the passage and pressed time in on me. We talked and leaned toward each other. I tried to read Marge and sensed her reading me. It was soft-voiced. Small anecdotes made big points. We spoke contrapuntally and never interrupted. Our hands brushed. We retained the contact. The pact was synchronous.

I said something funny. Marge laughed, displayed bad teeth and covered her mouth. I showed her my bad teeth. She laughed and held my chin to get a better look. I put my hand on her hand and steadied it. She said, Your teeth are worse than mine, and let her hand drop.

We looked away and gave the moment a breather. The train jiggled. We bumped. I brain-scrolled the script.

I instill confidence, she rebukes rashness, we consolidate our hurt. Dogs on the bed and warm nights in cold climates. Her older-woman status and insecurity. My assurance of how much I loved it. Her body's ripening currents over time. That eau de bath caught first thing in the morning.

The Bronxville stop approached. Marge and I shared a look. She said, I'm married.

I touched her shoulder and got up. Our knees brushed. My knees spasmed from the stunt with the cab. I got off the train, walked down the platform and stood by Marge's window. She pressed her hand up to her side of the glass. I placed my hand over it.

The brood den enclosed me. Caddy gigs and chump jobs kept me borderline solvent. I wrote and chased.

The sex-fiend cop became a hardback trilogy. The feminist poet was supplanted by a brainy call girl and the cop's resurrected ex-wife. The woman-with-a-cello book stayed in print. Ditto the my-mom-got-whacked-and-I'm-in-flight epic.

I was happy. I was grateful. I wrote books for minor remuneration and got minor acclaim. I was too circumspect to self-immolate and too tall and good-looking to lose. All my crazy shit stayed suppressed.

New York in the '80s. Jesus—what a fucking ride!!!!!

The stories and sustained sobriety saw me through. The stories were all a man meets a woman and now he moves on. They reflected my life as a minor artist and self-absorbed failure in love. New York City was felicitously female. It was a dizzying disproportion. The face pool was bottomless and bottomlessly reflecting. I kept seeing myself.

My prescience had deserted me. My spiritual aptitude had gone south. I had seen three brilliant women within moments early on. One had given me a precious vignette before her own vanishing. I saw women less discerningly now. Creative contentment had induced callousness. My psychic holes were patched with my books on shelves and the wound of Jean Hilliker stitched. The Curse had been roadblocked by hard work and a curt dismissal of the debt. I was out looking for women looking back and up at me.

My watcher's lifetime ran nearly four decades. My debilitating hunger was vaulted and lockboxed. I believed that it had given me mastery and an endless ticket to ride. Unbodied sex had almost proved fatal. I had sought death to prove my love to a ghost. It was the unconscious courting of reunion. I wanted to expunge our disparities and unite us as a whole.

I went at women because they were there and I wanted them. My revised standards denoted my flight from and back to the vault.

The stories I wrote controlled this self-phenomenon. I acceded to the strictures of the hard-boiled school and honed my craft. I perfected the art of womanizing simultaneously. I felt the weight of horrible circumstance upon me. It was huge. It did not justify my predation. I once scanned faces for rectitude. Now I read them for susceptibility to male charm.

One-night stands, short-term deals, longer-term girlfriends. Sex and no sex, brood sessions and phone calls. "No" was still "No"—but I heard it less and less. I was *that* attuned to female discontent.

I was a ruthlessly attuned listener and self-serving confidant. I was adept at dissecting devolving relationships and merciless in my critique of feckless men. Interrogator, interlocutor, pal. Rebuker of male weakness. The murdered mother's son. The feminist with the right-wing chivalry code. The demonizer of all misogynistic men. The guy who always wanted to get laid. The guy who always let the women lean in for the first kiss.

Fuck—the phone rang a lot. I kept a C-note tucked away for late-night cabs to the Apple. They were all decent women. No STDs, no coke-dealer boyfriends, no Glenn Close with a knife. They *loooved* my I-want-a-wife-and-daughters spiel. It was abstractly true. It was specifically and equally true that I didn't want it with *them*. I knew it going in. I shouldn't have lied. I'd possessed greater honesty in my unlaid and mystical state. I never bought their Let's-see-how-shit-plays-out routine. That permissive jive got kicked out of me in L.A. I capitulated to the notion for more sex and softness. I rejected it in my heart of hearts—and my heart of heart cradles my conscience.

If sex is to be everything, then so She must be. God kept saying that to me. *I did not bring you this far to drop you in an inappropriate bedroom. These women do not possess your ferocity. You'll know her if and when you meet her. Be assured that I love these less fierce women just as much as I love you.*

Stand back now. Sex is the investing of your full soul.

I know it more consciously now. The revelation often curtains my current time alone in the dark.

I ached for the kinship of the body then. I wanted every touch, taste and breath I could have. I was too compromised to ever let it be just like that.

I wanted an unnamed woman. It was the inextinguishable flame of my life. I wanted to write a specific woman's story. I *knew* her name: Elizabeth Short.

The Black Dahlia.

I had postponed the book. My debt to Betty Short intimidated me. I wrote six novels in breathless preparation. *I owed her.* I had to grant the woman a precious identity.

Betty Short died at 22. She was fatuous. She exemplified the silly-girl dreams indigenous to post-war America. *She* was *me.* She never got to outgrow her crazy shit and be somebody. She was all the Hancock Park girls with some fucked-luck chromosome inserted. She was all about invisibility. I never knew her, I never saw her, I only imagined her. I understood the male callousness and horrid pathology that mandated her demise. My predation provided the insight more than my mother's death did. My tender heart and smothering sense of conscience provided empathy. She died at 22. She was a kid. She was a wannabe actress with a chameleon personality and a penchant for telling whopping lies. She lied credibly on occasion. She had some knowledge of the limits of verisimilitude. She could have developed into a lie-for-profit storyteller. My depiction of Betty Short had to err on the side of honor glimpsed and foretold. She was visible in her invisibility. She died and spawned my kid crush and belated moral mandate. She preceded Joan, Karen and Erika and would in time lead them to me.

I owed Betty Short the romance of her life—and was determined to give it to her.

I began microfilm research and stitched up the plot. I recognized Jean Hilliker as a sister phantom reborn and dedicated the book to her. Honor the debt and reseal the tomb. Tell the story on your best-selling book tour. Combine Jean and Betty and ignore the enveloping issue of women. Seek more recent phantoms who might assuage you or at least fall for your act.

Marcia Sidwell and Marge from the train kept nudging me. They played hell with my phone-call stints and stunts with present women. I called directory assistance once a week and tried to track Marcia. I had a friend post a note at that L.A. Laundromat. I checked Grand Central Station for Marge. I cruised the Tarrytown station and lurked by the tracks. My landlady told me about the film *Brief Encounter*. It was a '45 British weeper. A man meets a woman in a train station. She's married, he's not. They acknowledge their love and kowtow to propriety and circumstance. My landlady said, You'd dig the sound track—it's all Rachmaninoff.

Bummer. You don't fold before circumstance. You're a weak sack of shit if you do.

True in 1985. Still true today.

Things were getting better. Book money trickled and almost flowed in. I tossed my caddy cleats. I wrote Betty's story as the phone did or did not ring.

And it was just that good and just that acclaimed. And it sold just that well. And it honored Jean Hilliker—as a fount of male inspiration and an *opportunity*.

People magazine ran a feature. The photos flattered me. I had a listed phone number. Four women called out of the blue.

Women #1 and #2 sounded crazy. I got off the line quick. I kowtowed to circumstance with the others. Beethoven grinned and scowled above us. Jesus, what a run! and You're a fucking *Scheisskopf*!

I always get what I want. It comes slow or fast and always costs a great deal.

The world veered toward me. Acknowledgment and compensation flowed. I bought women I'd just met four-figure cashmere sweaters. I overtipped waitresses to the verge of bankruptcy. I sent half the female universe flowers. Sex was there or was not there. I stayed in my dark basement with big bucks in the bank. The phone rang or did not ring. I wrote three more big historical books. Joan and Karen came of age a few miles south. Erika reached maturity a shouting distance away. They did not know one another or know me.

Propriety beckoned. Marriage and daughters became a fixation. I proposed to two women in short-term relationships. They vehemently declined. I proposed to a longer-term sweetheart. She said yes. I ran from her as we said our vows and settled in Hancock Park East.

Mary was a business executive. She hailed from big bucks in Akron, Ohio. She was a righteous human being and devoid of pretense. She represented a genetic brew of all the Hancock Park girls. I liked her very much. She got me a dog. I was tired. I was running out of inspired shit to tell women on the phone. We bought a big house in New Canaan, Connecticut. I thought marriage would *re-re-re-re-re*-suppress all my crazy shit. Mary told me that my nights in the dark might prove counterproductive in time. I conceded that she might have a point.

Our home was too spacious and airy. Marriage countermanded my shtick of seduce and explain. Cohabitation was constricting. Mary was in no way culpable. My office was too bright. My yard was too big. Mary was probity defined. She got me as much as women got me and played out her end of the string. I wanted out, so I got out. I had to be back in that dark hole, with a phone line plugged in.

Beethoven winked in welcome. Divorce was an exacting legal duty. Repentance came naturally. I saw the hasty union as atonable misconduct. Mary saw my departure as demons aswirl.

There's the dark, there's the phone, there's the Grosse Fugue.

"Take note of what you are seeking, for it is seeking you."

It's a paraphrase. Some swoony swami said it. Attribution doesn't matter, because it is true.

I always get what I want. I conjured her, so she came.

Lover, confidante, subverter, mighty soul and sacred comrade.

Hark the name Helen Knode.

PART III

COUGAR

8

The faces evaporated. The march of Them stopped at Her. She was sui generis. I took immediate note.

She slid into a booth at the Pacific Dining Car. Her journalist ex-boyfriend was interviewing me. I was jet-lagged and raw. My L.A. jaunts always scared me and confirmed my hometown retreat. Helen said she felt surreal. She was working off four tooth extractions and a painkiller buzz. God spoke to her. His message: you have not yet begun your life's work.

She was 33. She was small and fit. She wore slick-soled shoes and moved with deft pivots. She had light brown hair and blue eyes. Her glasses were too big. Her clothes were cut too trim. Don't dress monochrome. You said "God" unsolicited. Keep going on that.

I talked about myself. Helen hadn't heard of me. The ex-boyfriend tried to brief her. Helen acted bored. She wore too much lipstick. Take off your glasses and dig on me, please.

Chat meandered. Helen mentioned an East Berlin rendezvous. The wall was still up then. Her kraut lover blasted Beethoven's Ninth.

You said "Beethoven" unsolicited. Don't stop there. Take off your glasses. They overplay your face. They produce a circus-mirror effect.

The ex-boyfriend gobbled his steak. I ignored my food and eyeballed Helen. She complained about her teeth. She took off her glasses and rubbed her jaw.

There's the softness, there's the God sense, there's proportionate hurt and pizzazz.

I concocted some one-liners. They were all self-referential and all fell flat. Helen said she had to split. She cited a boyfriend and her sore gums. I stood up and thanked her for coming. Helen studied me.

The brood den was fall-winter cozy. I was completing a new novel and sharing bed space with my ex-dog. My ex-wife got custody. Barko bunked with me weekends. Women weren't calling me. My recent marriage had created a phone slump. I talked to my ex-wife's dog in the dark.

I miss Barko and look forward to our heavenly reunion. He was a homicidal bull terrier with an evil yen for human females. I gave him a *veeery* deep voice. We sprawled together and discussed Helen Knode.

The ex-boyfriend fed me the skinny. Barko and I riffed off the established facts.

She wrote for the *L.A. Weekly.* It was a counterculture rag fueled by lovelorn singles postings and prostitution ads. Helen's gig was bad-girl critic. She reviewed films, wrote features and penned a memoir column entitled "Weird Sister." It was tell-all/polemic. Attack the Right, decry gender bias, ballyhoo sex as politics.

Helen detailed her horny-huntress adventures. She hailed from western Canada. Her people were Texans in the oil biz. She was the eldest of four. Dad squandered the family fortune and pushed mom to Splitsville. Helen spent her late teen years in Kansas City and Lawrence. She lettered in tennis at KU. She got a master's degree at Cornell and played cowgirl cutup. Paris was next. Woo! Woo! It's Hurricane Hélène!

She's rugburned from rambunctious ruts and sordid sorties at the Sorbonne! She's fragging frisson-frazzled frogs en masse! She wears a black beret and mainlines espresso! She's the *diiiiirty* au pair girl! She's a bohemian-banging Bathsheba! She exhumes Existentialism as a one-wench show!

Four guys in one night? I dug it, but didn't want to believe it. Barko tormented me. You're pathetic, Dad! Helen was shagging schlong while you were jacking off on uppers!

I was less than obsessed and much more than tweaked. *Work* obsessed me. I was reliving L.A., '58. My corrupt-cop hero was torqued on a murderous carhop. She was equal parts ex-girlfriend Glenda and Swedish soprano Anne Sofie von Otter. I stared at a poster of the mesmeric mezzo and time-warped her to my book. Barko considered this pursuit unmanly.

Life was sweet. I retained my ex-wife's friendship and got Barko time. The alimony crunch didn't faze me. Helen lived on the left coast. Her Homeric-hung boyfriend was a minor impediment. Her ex-boyfriend said she was reading my books and was digging their romantic sweep. I read Helen's feature work and memoir *mishigas*. She was significantly good. God wanted her to jump-start her life's work. I knew what that was.

Marry me. Write a righteous crime novel. Co-opt the L.A. hipster-journalist scene. Critique present-day Hollywood and media culture. Portray your hatred for your boozed-out dad and your as-yet-undiscovered love for me. I'm God's conduit. Grasp this opportunity.

Spring '91. Cold nights and consoling darkness. The silent telephone. The demonic talking dog. Anne Sofie's lush lieder, sung directly to me. Helen Knode—raucous on my mind.

My book neared completion. Helen's ex-boyfriend requested another interview. I said, I'll fly out now. He said, The magazine won't cover it. I said, *I will.*

Helen moved first.

She'd read my last three books. She didn't know that the next book would be dedicated to her. *The Black Dahlia* wrecked her. The wantonness-versus-love motif did it. She grokked my weird-ass feminism. It inspired an idea: write a Dahlia-based cover piece for the *L.A. Weekly.* Her move: Will you show me around the sites?

She looked different that day. She was fresh-scrubbed and even more intent. She took off her glasses to frame close-ups. Her gaze was withering. L.A. was rain-damp. Helen wore jeans and boots. We toured the body-dump site and the Hollywood locations. Storm clouds brewed. I wanted to sit in Helen's car and wait out the longest thunderstorm in world history. I knew our heads and hearts would transport us solar-system wide.

It stayed dry. We trekked Beachwood Canyon, side by side. It was an effort. We both curbed a tendency to claim the lead. We talked. We monologued at similar length and rarely interrupted. My book on a dead woman gave us this world. I never said "Jean Hilliker" or "my mother." Helen went to abstraction as I held to anecdote. It challenged me. It made me ascribe meaning to my most-repeated tales. We discussed romanticism. Helen described the literary precedents. I ran down symphonic music. Content must dictate form. Form must be recognizable. Passion must never be squalid. Love must run in precise counterpoint to loss and death. That proportion stood as the basis of moral art. Helen said it first: All drama is a man meets a woman.

It had never been like this. I knew it then. Helen knew it in exact proportion.

We talked ourselves out on big ideas. We got lunch at a pita pit on Sunset. I calculated our age gap: nine years, four months, 12 days.

We were fried. Helen yawned and rubbed her eyes. They were steel blue. They importuned and demanded in perfect proportion.

Prosaic shit hovered. I had two more days in L.A. Helen's ex-boyfriend was throwing a bash the next night. Helen and her current boyfriend were invited. It vibed train wreck. I knew I'd create a scene. I sensed Helen sensing it.

The Dahlia day wound down. Our big talk cut through small talk to no talk. I did not deliver God's plan for Helen. I resisted the urge to propose.

Our good-byes were brusque. It was telepathy. We knew this: to address the day would be to affirm it and change our lives forever.

I slept poorly that night. The moon did funny things. I'd called my landlady back east. She said Barko had attacked the poster of Anne Sofie von Otter. I predicted Helen Knode's next three actions.

I knew she'd call me and bail on the party. I knew she'd cite her boyfriend. I knew she'd say, Where is this going?

I said, I'll write you a letter on the airplane. She said, I'll write you back.

Vows affirmed, call to honor, sacred pledge.

The correspondence began. We were constrained by distance and work commitments and wowed by the notion of an epistolary courtship. We utilized FedEx for a fast turn-around. Helen dumped her boyfriend. We were reinvesting in sex. Our letters set a lofty tone. There was no equivocation. We were comrades on a mission of unvanquishable love. That tone defined all our musings. Helen crafted the concept of B.C.E. and A.C.E. It meant "before the common era" and "after the common era." The Black Dahlia Day formed the dividing line. We viewed life as our personal adventure. Our preceding round-heeled stunts were auditions for a sizzling monogamy. We explored the gestalt of a man meets a woman. It was the hub of all our beliefs. We riffed on films, books, music and politics. Helen refused to pigeonhole me as a right-wing mystic. I poked at her bad-girl Marxism and got her to concede that she'd outgrown the pose. Our letters were breathless with what it all meant.

Nightly phone calls complemented our written texts. The banal-chat quotient ran zero. Sex was our low voices cloaked in collusion. The coastal gap allowed me to finish my new novel and yearn for Helen alone in the dark.

I bought a new Anne Sofie von Otter poster and kept Barko away from it. I brooded on Helen, to the exclusion of all other women. I re-read her letters, found new meanings and calibrated fresh responses. We spoke for hours at a pop. I laid out portentous epigrams. Helen cut loose with scattergun insight. She was smarter than I. It was intimidating. I lost my mental grounding and flailed for bright things to say. God threw us together. I believed it then and believe it no less vigorously now. I downplayed my religiousness and stressed a reluctant egalitarianism. Helen was a brain broiler. I was a caffeine-cooked autodidact in over his head. One thing consoled me: I knew God's big plan for Helen before she did.

I lacked her hyper-brilliance. She lacked my loony self-confidence and drive. I lacked her omnivorous view of the world in all its lively flux. She lacked my brutal will.

That astonishing spring. Passion postponed. Palpitating souls eternally entwined.

· · ·

We collided at the airport. Our embrace scorched baggage claim. Helen's hair looked darker. Tears washed her eyes an even paler blue.

We kissed in her car. Airport cacophony drowned out my heartbeat. I was tantrically tapped and two-months tumescent. L.A. looked all new. It was *our* town more than *my* town now. I reserved us a suite at the Mondrian Hotel. It was my favorite local brood spot. I wanted to desaturate my images of all other women with Helen Knode right there.

The valet-park guys knew me and dug me. I over-tipped and exuded big-white-bwana savoir faire. I laid on the largesse. The guys called me "Jefe." The desk fag whizzed us upstairs.

Helen whooped at the suite and whooped at my gauche white-trash glee. We gobbled honor-bar almonds and ran to the bed. It wasn't anything I had predicted, fantasized, sound-tracked or brain-screened before. Helen's hands on my face reframed my whole life.

Draped windows darkened us and eclipsed the Sunset Strip. Time did a funny lust-bunker thing. Locations and climates merged. I lost track of all the things I planned to say. Lovemaking and talk got twisted into a slow-burning fuse. My mind went blank as I counted the moles on Helen's back. We tossed a pillow on the bedside clock. Street noise subsided to a purr.

We found robes and cracked the curtains for some face-reading light. Dusk backlit Helen in mid-laugh. I said, "Will you marry me?" Helen whooped and said, "Yes, I will."

So you found Her.

What does it mean?

Where does it take you?

It means everything. It takes you everywhere. You follow her lead.

My credo: Expect nothing, risk everything, give all. Helen's rejoinder: Yes, assume risk. You will gain or lose commensurate with your deepest consciousness and the purity of your intent.

I felt cleansed. Helen's joy was emancipation. She stamped the deed to The Curse "paid in full" and dared me to dance to her tune.

It was a Baby-I'm-gonna-make-you-mine oldie. She pulled it out of a circa '60 slush pile. It bid me to re-spin my compulsive appetite and dig on it as happiness expressed.

I'd been happy before. It was always manifestly urgent. I always wanted more and knew I'd always get it. A hollow thunk kicked around in me and kept me vigilant, nonetheless. Hyper-acuity alerts opportunists to the presence of more. *More* was now moribund. Helen Knode had rendered it *Less*.

Lover, confidante, sacred comrade. Satirist, debunker and funny motherfucker.

Nobody had ever *reallllly* gotten me. Nobody had ever *reallllly* gotten her. Our imaginations merged. Our zests for life overlapped and coalesced. Helen Knode and James Ellroy—*that's entertainment*!

We looked *gooooood* together. We exemplified yucks and fucks with refinement. We loved life and lived to laugh. We were *fuuuuunny*. We were always concocting hilarious shit.

Helen messed with my memory. She de-genderized it. I forgot female faces seen and recalled, girls stalked and B&E'd. Helen recast iconic figures and demoted them to bit roles. Marcia Sidwell and the wish-named Joan? Now synaptic flotsam. Helen's message: I'm here, they're not. Let's make love and laugh.

The world was fair comic game. Ditto, her family and friends and a backwash of our ex-lovers. Helen's act complemented my talking-dog shtick and race routines. Helen's character was manifest. It allowed her political wiggle room. She dug my right-wing spiels and scolded me through excessive repetitions. We ping-ponged between the comedy hour and *looooong* talks on what it all meant.

We scheduled our wedding for fall '91 and rented a house in Laurel Canyon. Helen bowed to my desire for a Christian service and stipulated a female pastor. The woman disliked me. She told Helen that our union would not last—because I had darty eyes.

I met Helen's family. I liked them fine and dominated them with a bullying exuberance. Helen was complicit. I brought out the class clown in her. I didn't know from families. Their social codes and clash of egos vexed me. I ballyhooed myself and extolled Barko's antics. Barko sold dope to the brothers in southside L.A. Barko edited *Snout* magazine. Barko whacked JFK and got Jackie all for himself. The Knodes laughed through their shock and did a "Boy, Helen's met her match" number. Helen kicked me when my shtick failed to fly.

Issues percolated. I had a sweet three-book deal and wanted to glom a pad in Connecticut. I loved the East Coast and craved access to Barko. Helen was reluctant. The East reeked of the deep tsuris of her Cornell grad school days. L.A. was her town now. I couldn't live in that ghost zone. Helen agreed to the move. It invigorated me. I delivered God's plan for her.

She *got* it. The crime novel, the female journo in duress. The hated father, a botched patricide, the cop-lover redolent of *me*. Brilliant Helen: she heard me out and started popping plot points within minutes. I knew she'd excel at the task.

Summer '91. Warm nights and the overfurnished love shack. The moment I turned 43 years, two months and seven days of age and outlived Jean Hilliker.

Helen said I would outlive her influence. Our union was proof positive. I had chosen to forsake traumatic drive and compulsion for joy. I had fictionally replicated the redhead. My cast of '50s women were *of* her and *served* her as vessels of acknowledgment. My job now: seek groovy happiness—with H. M. Knode.

Which I did.

I dubbed Helen the "Cougarwoman." She was sleek, tawny and indigenous to the western plains. She was conversant with outré religions and grokked their animal worship. She called me "Big Dog," because I loved dogs and bayed extemporaneously. My dog-den mentality unnerved her. I lived to be alone with her or plain alone in tightly structured spaces. I craved containment. I viewed other people as interlopers and den crashers. I wanted to contain our relationship and four-wall it. It was wild-ass one-on-one. The exclusive nature sandbagged my long-standing fixation with having a brood of daughters. Helen didn't rule out children. It was put on indefinite hold. Passion ruled our immediate moments.

Summer '91. Weekend jaunts to Santa Barbara. We always ate at a joint called Paul Bhalla's Cuisine of India. It was always empty or close to it. That gored me. The place felt talismanic and linked to our fate. I did not want that restaurant to tank or close. We had to be able to go back and thwart the passage of time there. Helen always sat to my left. She always took her glasses off and made her eyes kaleidoscopes. Fear slammed me then. *I must never lose this woman. Please, God. Don't let her die or let anything rip us apart.*

Our wedding: 10/4/91. Two rooms at the Pacific Dining Car.

Helen wore a pink-peach '40s vintage dress. I wore my ancestral kilt. Helen looked stunningly cougarlike and hip/feral. The pastor performed our hybrid vows. I got Christian lip service and Helen got lots of New Age woo-woo. The pastor glared at me, but did not mention my darty eyes. I tagged her as a pissed-off dyke.

Helen's family flew in from Kansas and Texas. My publishing friends flew in from New York. Some old buddies from AA showed. The toasts ran heartfelt and slightly off-color. Helen tossed out zingers like "hot cougar love" and quoted Doris Lessing: "Marriage is sex and courage." I threw out a mock-impromptu rock song, replete with lurid lyrics. Helen whooped and busted me to the guests. "That's a retread, Big Dog! You wrote that for one of your ex-bitches!"

Steak dinners off the menu and a custom wedding cake. Cross-table chitchat while Helen worked the room and I withdrew into my head. I brain-tripped. Jean Hilliker would have been 76 years, five months and 19 days old had she lived.

Helen pirouetted, her dress swirled, a few of her male friends whistled. I got evil mad and sent out shitty looks. Helen caught my eye, smiled and brought me down in a heartbeat.

Please, God, don't let this end.

Please, God, let us ascend to you at the same instant.

Helen recharted my brainscape. She heard all my stories and demanded new interpretations. She respectfully requested sex yarns. I recast all my previous lovers as buffoons and Knode wannabes. Helen was less disingenuous. She layered in the good sex and donkey-dicked dudes and got me angry and jealous. I wanted to control her life's narrative. It had to be properly titillating *and* anoint Helen as saintlike. I pressed Helen for revisions and got the single one I craved: Before you, it was all puerile and trifling.

Ubiquity.

Helen was flat-out alive. Jean Hilliker was the entomber. My mother ghost-danced through dark rooms and encouraged me to scroll faces. Helen cracked the blackout curtains and let me glimpse the light outside.

We moved back to New Canaan, Connecticut. My ex-wife and ex-dog lived a few miles away. Helen dug the greenbelt aspect and hated the surrounding urbanism. I bullied her there. Our tidal-wave courtship came with a price. The move ripped her away from her family and friends. The move dumped her in a hostile burb with a familyless man and a talking ex-dog. I levied a jive male mandate. We have to live here, that's the bottom line, you'll get used to it. The fucked-up subtext: A man's gotta do what a man's gotta do.

New Canaan remained Hancock Park East. My ex-wife remained a composite of the prep school girls I'd prowled and peeped years back. I lured Helen to a reconstructed memory zone. She subverted my relationship to my past as we lived a re-creation of it.

She was homesick. She ragged New Canaan as she torch-songed L.A. She'd moved for a man. It rankled her feminism. Manhattan brought back her wild days as an East Village journo. She was past all that kid shit now. The East torqued her as it cradled me.

We settled in. Helen began work on her novel. I compiled notes on a political epic. It was my first non-L.A.-set fiction. I saw L.A. as a dark room I couldn't revisit. I wanted all my memory spaces compartmentalized. I viewed my new marriage as a legal document that expunged our collective past. Special provisos allowed us to exploit it for dramatic purposes and titillation. I had misread women many times before. I had superimposed my single-mindedness and go-go ethos upon them. Helen possessed it already. I knew that then. She possessed a more refined version of my drive and could integrate the world within it. I know that now. She was attempting to provide me with a stable overall life and a balanced day-to-day existence. I rolled over for her charm, wit and passion. I resisted the moment-to-moment toil of domestic duty. I abrogated my responsibilities along gender lines. I could not wash dishes or vacuum floors and left those jobs to Helen. I saw no point in social outings. They entailed other people and often bid me to rude behavior. Helen was Her, She, The Other. She had countermanded Jean Hilliker adroitly. We were united in pursuit of a divine efficacy. Our purpose was to sustain each other and create big art. Our love would see us through the performance of our sacred duty. The more circumscribed our world, the more direct our point A to point B journey.

That was my mission statement. It was not Helen Knode's. I did not inflict it upon her as a philosophy or a step-by-step task. I saw it as a logical expression of our great romantic adventure. Helen was considerably more flexible and viewed my agendas as liberating in intention and often restricting in practice. I lived with the woman who was then the great love of my life. I bopped in and out of My World and Our World on an ad hoc basis.

Helen's physical presence and surety juiced my creative engine. My brain cells popped in an effort to keep up with her. My blinders fit more securely and cut off the female spirits always clouding my peripheral view. There was She, there was Me, there was Women relinquished as Obsession. Helen Knode was inherently delightful. It sugarcoated her critique of my abysmal social skills, barnyard table manners and household helplessness. Helen was hilarious—even when pissed off. She called me "Big Dog" with love and "Zoo Animal" in exasperation. Low fury bubbled within her and occasionally popped into rage. She revered my maleness. She glimpsed dark domestic dimensions early on.

I was impervious, imperious, oblivious. The manifestations were all preposterously male. I could earn big dough, but not read credit-card bills or balance checkbooks. I dug good chow, but refused to cook. I made exultant animal sounds in the john and treated the place as my personal trough. I grandstanded at family gatherings or skulked off to read sports-car magazines and brood in the dark. Social gigs left Helen frayed-wire tense. I pulpit-pounded and baited her left-leaning friends. I seized up around other men and dominated them with glares, right-wing barbs and general rancor. Helen nursed that low fury and blew up on occasion. I repented on occasion and reneged on my vows to change.

It was easy to repent and easier to renege. I saw Helen's beefs as small when compared to the big blast of US. I was blithely disrespectful. It dishonored our marriage. I know it now. I didn't know it then.

The Big Blast was all-encompassing. I felt safe and provided safety for a transcendent woman. Our daily rapport was astonishingly quick-witted and grounded in the big idea of the sacred ride of life. I turned Helen on to boxing and watched her become a rabid fan. We went to piano recitals at Carnegie Hall. Helen fed me drafts of her personal wisdom and watched me work them into my worldview. We went to films and further anthropomorphized Barko—New Canaan's K-9 King.

We wrote books in separate rooms, under one roof. Helen attacked the discipline of the crime novel with cougarlike tenacity, native skill and Knodeian konviction. She pulsingly persevered. It thrilled me and vouched my great faith in her. She never took my name. She remained a Knode and not an Ellroy. I'm a matriarchalist now. I wasn't then. I wasn't yet a Hilliker in my soul. I watched Helen write her way out of my shadow—as I worked triple overtime to make that shadow grow.

The political novel had incubated pre-Helen. It derived from my conscious decision to dump L.A. as my sole fictional locale. The preceding L.A. Quartet was my hometown elegy and another giant contain–Jean Hilliker compartment. Those books were all Bad Men In Love With Strong Women. Those books reeked of A Man Meets A Woman—as historical L.A. intercedes and demands that they change. Four novels, one Beethovenian manifesto. Fictional infrastructures complementing large public events. Earthquake combustions of physical love defining *everything* therein.

I was obsessed with *women* then. The emotional text was preordained. I was in love with *one woman* now. My whole world swerved. I got de- and re-compartmentalized. Helen rendered all other women sterile. My all-new novel got de-sexualized.

And more sophisticated and colder. And more about ruthless men and self-seeking solitude.

I know it now. I didn't know it then.

Helen took me in and provided shelter. My life was blessedly contained. It comforted me. The restrictions impinged on Helen. I had a safe place to work and brood. Containment means suppression. Suppression festers and explodes in the end. Helen bought me time. It allowed me to go insane at a slow and highly productive pace.

Crazy boy, you still don't know, no woman can save you.

9

You're working too hard.

Helen kept saying it. I kept calling my energy a by-product of US. Suburban life and blissful monogamy. The groovy ex-dog. One woman instead of *women.* You have to dig *that.*

Helen was skeptical. We're not making love like we used to. You've become disembodied. You're always off in your head.

I rebuffed her first few salvos. I denied the presence of sexual stasis and pledged instant redress. Helen's candor unnerved me. I felt like I'd trashed our romantic code and abridged our marital vows. Sex was everything. We both believed it. We were two years in. I rejected the marriage-as-complacency saw. Helen rejected it with the same fervor. I stonewalled Helen's suggestion of looming dysfunction. There's trouble in paradise. Don't tell me this.

Shit, there's seepage. One compartment's fissured now. Fuck, *I'm happy.* I'm writing a new novel. I'm living big history at a trillion rpms. I'm devotedly in love with you. I may be approaching contentment. Please don't hit me with this—*yet.*

That was my rationale. It was halfway true. The other half was more problematic. I was a cut-and-run guy pre-

Helen. I never got to this point before. This is where we confront and surmount. Please don't make me do it—*yet.*

And I'm tired of chasing and seducing. And my erotic fire has embered and weirdly re-flamed. My book is a scorching blaze. Now sex is power and power is fiction and fiction has replaced sex. Darling, it's all tangled. I only want to be with you. Let's not broach this—*yet.*

The men in my novel were power-mad. The men in my novel were dissemblers and compartmentalizers. They were me sans all conscience and the guidance of Helen Knode. Helen Knode personified an exponential shift in my thinking. Helen Knode's counsel led me to write a new kind of book. Helen Knode saved me from my gender-wide crush on women. Helen Knode got to the truth before I did in most cases. Now she got me to *this.*

Please, Cougar—not *yet.*

I ran, I postponed, I diverted, I crawled back in my head. Infrequent liaisons sealed the compartment. The fissures contracted and held.

American Tabloid was the private nightmare of public policy. The infrastructure was power grab in place of love as redemption. Women veered through the book in subordinate roles. This was emblematic of the early '60s. I wanted to write an all-new kind of novel and incinerate my ties to L.A. The former was laudable, the latter was not. L.A. made me. Jean Hilliker was killed there. I met Helen Knode a block from where I was born. The book was almost finished. Helen kept saying, *You're working too hard.*

Christmas '93 approached. Helen had written a draft of her book and gave me pages to read. They were impressive and raw by my inflated standards. I ladled on a line edit and Ellroyized the prose. Helen laughed at the loony language loops and tossed the pages back in my face.

The toss-back was loving. We laughed about it then. I

cut Knodeisms and juked the text with macho-maimed *mishigas*. I did not feel rancorous *then*. I'll post-date and dissect my animus *now*.

I was running from the marriage. I wanted to parry Helen's where's the sex? routine. I was back in my dark-room mode, minus the constant Beethoven and chicks on the phone. I was the shirker and Helen was the confronter. Our domestic drama was starting to swerve along standard gender lines. I found that repellent. My tory feminism was playing out as a shuck. Helen had become the moral leader of our union. Her wisdom and courage superseded mine. My job was to retreat from my productive mania and give her all of myself once again.

I couldn't do it.

I didn't know *how* to do it.

I didn't know that I *should* do it and *had* to do it—*yet*.

Then The Curse took an all-new form and Jean Hilliker bought us some time.

We exchanged gifts Christmas morning. I gave Helen a cashmere sweater and a tweed blazer. Helen gave me a fleece-lined bomber jacket. Barko got a shitload of beef-dipped bones.

Helen pointed to the last package. It was rectangular and festively wrapped.

She said the gift required some research. She expressed trepidation. She said, I hope you won't be upset.

I unwrapped the package. I felt the frame and saw black-and-white flickers behind glass. I instantly knew what it was.

The *L.A. Times* photo. Quickly dismissed in '58. Unher-alded that Christmas. Frequently reproduced and perhaps over-scrutinized now.

I'm a doofus ten-year-old. I'm wearing a plaid shirt and light-colored pants. My zipper is prophetically half-down. A cop just said, "Son, your mother's dead."

Helen always cuts to the punch line. She asked me what I was thinking *then* and what I was thinking *now*.

I said, "Opportunity."

I had a magazine-feature gig within weeks and a book deal a month later. My first job: view Jean Hilliker's murder file and describe the jolt. My second: hire a homicide cop, attempt to solve the case and write an investigative autobiography.

The Curse was a formal summons of death and a bidding to engage the world obsessed. This new codicil empowered me to again exploit misfortune. I had to contain the Hilliker/Ellroy journey as a crime tale. It was a specious task at the get-go. Jean Hilliker and I comprise a love story. It was born of shameful lust and shaped by the power of malediction. Our ending was not and could never be the apprehension of a killer and a treatise on the victim-killer nexus. My precocious sexuality pre-shaped The Curse and preordained the resolution as my overweening desire for women.

I *knew* we would not find the killer. I *knew* my murder memoir would portray an arc of reconciliation and lockbox Jean Hilliker anew. I was deliriously willful and callow in 1994. I believed that all resolutions could be contained within narrative form. Helen knew otherwise. She gave me the picture so that I might view it in wonder and benefit in indefinable ways. She added mitigating clauses to The Curse without knowing that The Curse existed. Helen contended then, and still contends, that I always write my way through to the truth. She believes that I rarely get it right the first time and that I often impose form at the expense of content. She knew that Jean Hilliker was more than a murder victim and less than a fount of rapturous worship. She sent me out to grasp at verisimilitude—in the hope it would sustain and enrich both of us.

I lived in Los Angeles for fifteen months. I talked to Helen every night. We had several East Coast/West Coast reunions and got back fractions of sex here and there. I was always anxious and distracted. Sex had always been pursuit and the performance of the task. My years with Helen had illuminated that and had pushed me tenuously past it. Awareness does not equal spontaneity in bed. My current task was to play detective and frame my mother within book pages.

I read ancient police files and compiled notes. I partnered up with a brilliant ex-cop named Bill Stoner. We interviewed scores of elderly barflies, East Valley riffraff and retired policemen. We got a great deal of TV and newspaper play. All our work got us nowhere. We lived the dead-end/unsolved-crime metaphysic. I brooded in the dark with Rachmaninoff and Prokofiev. The music described romanticism's descent into twentieth-century horror. It complemented my psychic state. I knew we'd never find the killer. I took copious notes on my emerging mental relationship with my mother. I understood that the force of my memoir would derive from a depiction of that inner journey. I erred in that regard. I knew that reconciliation was the only proper ending as I signed my book contract. I learned very little about Jean Hilliker's death. I gained considerable knowledge about her life and structured my revelations in a salaciously self-serving manner.

I was her, she was me, we were doppelgangers and mirrored souls in duress.

I believed it then. I consider it fraudulent and dramatically expedient now. I differentiated her with some minor details and let the convenient and viable theme of oneness stand as the truth. I did not acknowledge the calculated maliciousness of The Curse or reveal that I would never know Jean Hilliker as long as I sought atonement in women.

The investigation continued. *American Tabloid* was published midway through. It was a smash. I book-toured and deftly segued from doomed mom to doomed JFK. The lease on the Connecticut pad expired. Helen and I considered our options and decided to move to Kansas City. She had family there. I dug the high-swank pockets around Ward Parkway. We flew in and purchased a six-bedroom Tudor crib. Man-o-Manischewitz—it was Hancock Park on growth hormones!!!

Helen did all the relocation shit work. I waltzed in and waltzed back out to brood and play cop. My absence enraged Helen. She teethed on it. Our daily phone talks were rife with her resentment and my halfhearted repentance.

The investigation was boring me. I had everything I needed to write the book. Jean Hilliker had been reconsidered, recast and realigned with my orbit. I was mentally tapped out on her. My orbit shifted. I got realigned with the faces.

They came at me. I didn't seek them out. It was an unconscious re-migration. My exchange of marital vows carried a binding no-fantasy clause that rendered me mentally as well as physically faithful. I was just that rigorous and disciplined. The gutter-to-stars arc of my life and its overall extremity had convinced me of the wisdom of absolutism and the folly of permissiveness. *I had to be that way.* I was a man of devout faith. Psychologizing was a slothful substitute for the iron-willed pursuit of perfection. I was heedless, reckless, boorish, domineering and self-involved. I knew it and made sporadic attempts to eradicate it in practice. Character flaws were compartments. Compartments fissured and seeped. I acknowledged that, tenuously. I possessed two paramount spiritual goals and held them as unassailable compartments. They were my loyalty to my craft and to Helen Knode. I gave them my entire conscious focus. I underestimated the reflexive power of suppression and all the crazy shit that lies dormant inside your head.

The Faces.

The Women.

Them.

I was burned out on Jean Hilliker. I had melded her into my craft with all the guile and Curse-derived passion I then possessed. My marriage was compartments within compartments, all starting to crack. I quadrupled my nightly prayers for Helen and grasped at the compartment of physical chastity with suffocating force.

It's all right, Cougar—there's only you—they're just spirits aflame.

There's Marcia Sidwell at the Laundromat and Marge on the train. There's Rachmaninoff's Second Piano Concerto from *Brief Encounter.* There's the wish-named Joan as she was then and might be now. She still feels prophetic. I'm nine years away from the real Joan, with her stunning, gray-streaked hair. There's Karen out of my circa '80 rainy-night dream. She's more than a decade away in true life. Erika will find me in the backwash of both women.

And all the others. Alive in blur and hyper-focus. Indistinguishable spirits—each and every one unique.

I secured a new Anne Sofie von Otter poster. I propped it up on my work desk and studied her face. It was arrogant and kind in an artist's proportion. She was blond and fair. Her hair was square-cut and severe and expressed the force of her will. She had rough skin and refused to disguise it.

That displayed her composure, merged with a big gulp of diva's Fuck you.

She was seven years, two months and five days younger than I. A classical music guide told me that. I found a full-length photo. She was lush-bodied and seemed to be quite tall. I bought some lieder recordings and went crazy with her voice.

I cried. I got up close to the poster and hugged a pillow. I couldn't understand her words sung in German. I improvised my own English love lyrics and studied her face. The poster was affixed beside my mother's murder file. I trembled and knocked it over sometimes.

The music, her picture, the meaning transposed.

I was threatened by her genius. She was threatened by mine. We were big and strong and full of lovers' fight. We were horrified by our loneliness and appalled by our need and went out in the world with our crazy beauty just to get a touch of it back.

We burned down rooms. We knew what everything meant. We understood terror and fury as no one else had. It hurt to be together and hurt more to be apart. Our mouths clashed. Our teeth scraped. Our arms ached from the meld. We knew each other's smells and heard each other's voices and told each other things that no one else ever had.

Hear me, Helen. I was not disloyal. They're all sacred chords that play out faint and let me return to you, chaste.

10

You're working too hard.

Helen kept saying it. She said it first in '93. She kept it up through '99. No sex simmered as an issue, intermittently expressed.

Helen always broached it. I always said, "Soon, babe," or "I'm on deadline," or "You know we'll get it back." Helen mollified me or looked gut-shot or blank-faced let it rest. Her critique of my domestic forfeit assumed an edge. She called herself the "Concierge." I was the "Star Boarder" or "VIP Guest." She was the "Zoo Animal's Keeper."

I admitted that I was overbooked and cited her dogged work on her novel. It bought me a few grudging concessions and more time to brood and work.

Our life was adrenalized and outwardly sweet. Kansas City was the white-trash comfort zone I had always creamed for. I was a local celeb. Ex-dog Barko was back east with my ex-wife. Our new bull terrier, Dudley, possessed Barkoesque panache. *My Dark Places* was a bestseller and got a slew of year-end nods. The film *L.A. Confidential* reaped boocoo awards and got me big ink. Helen hunkered down, honed and re-honed her book. I read several drafts and did not intrude on the text. It was a bonaroo crime story set in a metaphysically re-mapped

L.A. Helen persisted. She was the Cougarwoman. Big ideas were her prey.

You're working too hard.

Yes, you're right.

I was brooding up the sequel to *American Tabloid*. It was conceived as my massive take on the American '60s. I had a feature-magazine contract. It mandated hours of daily work and near-constant travel. I hustled some choice screenwriting gigs and stretched myself ultra-thin. I worked, worked and worked. Helen and I shared meals and bumped shoulders in hallways. Dudley liked her more than me. He was diffident in my presence. He had me pegged as a head-tripper and a negligent dad.

I was gone a lot. Film and magazine work boinged me to L.A. and back. I stayed in the high-end hotels I'd drooled for in my childhood. I cut the lights and conjured Anne Sofie.

We talked. She always stretched out on my left and tossed a leg over me. I kissed her arms and shoulders. She told me things I never knew about music. I told her things she never knew about books. She riffed on her travel woes and fruit entourage. She said, *You're working too hard.*

I admitted it. I was more candid with my fantasy lover than I was with my wife. Anne Sofie described my symptoms. She lay entwined with me. She knew my rhythms and felt my skewed chemistry.

You sleep poorly, you mumble, you take shallow breaths. You're always checking your limbs for cancer bumps that aren't really there. You stare into mirrors and count the flecks in your eyes. Liebchen, *they're just natural flaws. You're not going blind.*

Anne Sofie consoled me. She put her face up to mine and showed me the flecks in *her* eyes. I got scared and asked Helen to affirm my robust health. She stage-sighed and rolled her eyes. She said, "You're fine, Big Dog" or *"You're working too hard."*

The work kept pressing, the phone kept ringing, I kept saying yes. My pace was Herculean. My focus was Draculean. My design for the new novel was super-planetary. I read research briefs and compiled notes. The outline ran 345 pages. I foresaw a 1000-page manuscript and a 700-page hardback.

America: four years, five months and 17 days of wild shit. Two hundred characters. Comparatively few women and a reduced romantic arc. An abbreviated style that would force readers to inject the book at my own breathless rate.

I wanted to create a work of art both enormous and coldly perfect. I wanted my standard passion to sizzle in the margins and diminish into typeface. I wanted readers to know that I was superior to all other writers and that I was in command of my claustrophobically compartmentalized and free-falling life.

Hubris, arrogance, isolation. The novel as sensory assault. The neglect of my dearly beloved wife.

Head-tripper. Absentee husband. Furious führer and furtive fantasist.

I had Anne Sofie. I had Anne Manson, the K.C. Philharmonic conductor. I had a lesbian FedEx driver. I had the wish-named Joan, aged to 50-plus. The real Joan turned 34 that Halloween.

Fever dream.

My nerves accelerated and my insomnia increased. They were locked in sync with the pace of history fantastically revised. I wrote *The Cold Six Thousand* in 14 months. I was ever the racist provocateur and cleaved to the souls of my right-wing assassins. I was rarely a real-life or fictional lover and boarded at the luxe hotel of my chaste chum Helen. I spent a great deal of time alone in the dark with Anne Sofie.

I was triumphantly exhausted. I completed the book and expected to feel a resultant buoyancy. I was mistaken. My nerves continued to crackle at history's mad pace.

My agent and publisher praised the book and considered it a crowning achievement. Helen disagreed. She called it overlong, overplotted, and reader un-friendly. She said it was jittery and frayed and approximated my spiritual state.

You're working too hard, Big Dog. Get some rest now.

A mega book tour loomed. Five European countries and 32 U.S. cities, consecutively. Months away from home and continual travel. Interviews, press conferences and nightly bookstore events. A long stint as *le grand fromage*.

Pre-publicity gigs loomed: long-lead magazine profiles, culture-TV, an Ellroy cable doco. A big excerpt spread synced to pub date. It boiled down to a Brutha, you de Man moment. I wanted to ride it, rock it, roll it, groove it, grok it, grab it and grasp it for all it was worth.

I prepared for the ego onslaught. My sleep came and went. I fixated on benign skin lesions and prayed off a fear of carcinogenic assault. I went on long head trips with Anne Sofie, Anne Manson and the lezbo FedEx babe. I spent hours perfecting my reading gigs and podium patter. I bought some snazzy new threads to enhance my You de Man status.

Helen's book was almost done. Her agent's plan was to auction it during my book-tour summer. Our sex stasis remained an acknowledged, but still tightly buttressed compartment. My plan was to wring my tour dry and watchdog the sale of Helen's book. *Then* we would make time to reemerge as flesh and blood man and wife.

France, Italy, Holland, Spain, Great Britain. Conquer the Continent and annihilate the Isles. Ambush America and traipse a triumphant trail back to your wife.

Bon voyage, Big Dog. I won't say "Don't work too hard," just "Remember to rest."

Blooey.

It started instantly. A wave of discomfort hit me on the airplane. Short breaths, pins-and-needles poings, sweats. A business-class aisle seat, good legroom, a loose seat belt. Claustrophobic compression at 30,000 feet.

I tried to write it off. It was anticipation born of huge achievement and joy. I couldn't sustain the thought. Acute vigilance swamped it.

I ignored the seat belt sign and jammed to the john. I spent 20 minutes looking for rips and tears in my eyes. The stewardess knocked. I told her I was all right. My bladder swelled. I took a long piss and became convinced that I had diabetes. I rolled up my sleeves and examined a spot for metastasization. My bowels swelled. I defecated and became convinced that I had colon cancer. The stewardess knocked again and told me people were waiting. I tremble-walked out of the john. I was sweaty, my fly was down, passengers eyed me weird.

Six more hours to Paris.

Dinner gave me a task. My bladder and bowels settled and blitzed my earlier diagnoses. I ate a third of my dinner and lost my appetite. I got an ancient brain signal to guzzle scotch and prayed it away. I could not rewire my brain past catastrophe. I could not physically or mentally unclench or deactivate my antennae. I could not focus on the upcoming blast of big-time acclaim. I fixated on immanent bodily malfunction and scanned the seat rows for potential assailants.

I shut my eyes and tried to relax. My thumping heartbeat popped my eyes open. I checked my arms for cancer signs under the seat lamp. My panic wavered and fluttered during a full-hour scan. I shut my eyes and prayed for a final medical verdict. I opened my eyes and saw a gray-haired woman walk back to her seat.

She felt like a divine signal. I craned my neck and furtively watched her for the rest of the flight.

My publisher gave me my arrival day off. Paris in spring—who gives a shit? Travel bored me then and bores me now. Sightseeing and the gourmet life were for geeks, freaks and fruitcake artistes. I holed up in my hotel suite. I pulled the curtains and got three hours of strange, pass-out sleep. I woke up, unrested. I spent an hour at the bathroom mirror, examining my eyes. I reached a tenuous accord: your vision is fine. My publisher called with great news: the book zoomed to #2 on the *Le Monde* best-seller list. I got a two-second joy jolt and started studying my arms.

Helen called. I ran down my symptoms and got her seal of good health. The *Le Monde* coup jazzed her. She wanted to dwell on it. I got bombarded by images of the woman on the plane.

Helen bid me adieu. I guzzled coffee to redistribute my exhaustion and stimulate myself someplace safe. I ate a piece of fruit and a roll to recirculate the buzz. Heavy curtains kept the suite dark. I stretched out on the bed and boomeranged.

Anne Sofie. The airplane woman. Real and fictive images merged with narrative—all day and all night, back and forth.

I couldn't sleep, I couldn't unclench, I couldn't forge a truce with my monkey brain and simply rest. I started thinking, What if this doesn't stop?

. . .

It continued.

I performed brilliantly throughout.

My book was a sales smasheroo and a critic's mixed bag. The smart frogs cautiously praised the book and echoed Helen Knode's doubts. The Ellroy-toady frogs culture-vultured them out. I jaunted through France with my editor, translator and publicist. I gave interviews, attended lunches and dinners and never missed a beat. Bookstore gigs and late meals went past midnight. I engaged the iron-willed pursuit of perfection and never publically succumbed.

My colleagues saw me running gaunt and jaggedy. My public did not. No one saw me fixating on cell formations that microscopes could not detect. No one saw my hour-long eye exams. No one saw me run to mirrors to scrutinize eroding flesh.

I called Helen every night. She buoyed me and blitzed my fear for the moments that we spoke. I wrapped myself dark with Anne Sofie and the airplane woman. I rewrote her life.

She was a Jewish college professor. She was as religious as I was in her own faith. She was divorced and had a daughter in college. The daughter was a fine young woman in every regard. I had long talks with her. She indulged my long-yearned-for fatherhood and barely tolerated my pedagogy. The woman and I talked and made love. She tossed one leg over me, the way Anne Sofie did.

The real Joan was Jewish and a college professor. The real Joan and I had wanted a daughter. The real Joan bore a child without me finally. I swear that I unconsciously summoned her in curtain-dark bedrooms that spring. I swear that the summons was issued as an antidote to The Curse.

I couldn't sleep, I barely slept, I unstintingly did my job. Little noises became amplified—incremental volume jumps every day. I weaved through Charles de Gaulle Airport and caught a flight to Italy.

Spring in Roma—who gives a shit? My publisher booked me a boss hotel suite and gave me the night off. I pulled the curtains and anchored them with heavy chairs. I had an epiphany and began reading the Gideon Bible placed in the nightstand drawer.

I got halfway through the Old Testament. Cancer cells started eating at me.

I ran to the bathroom and scratched my arms bloody. I doused them with rubbing alcohol and intensified the sting. I convinced myself that caustic agents had killed all the cells. I read the Bible until I passed out.

This madness was my whole world now. It was entirely real as it transpired. I did not second-guess it or retreat from my duty.

I did interviews in a hotel salon and smiled for photo shoots. The cancer cells returned during my first-day lunch break. I slipped a bellman a C-note. He drove me to a dermatologist quicksville. The doctor spoke English. He examined my arms and told me I didn't have cancer. He called it a minor rash exacerbated by scratching and prescribed a soothing skin cream.

The book was a smash in Italy. I charmed journalists and the book-buying public shitless. My colleagues said, Ciao, baby, and packed me off to Holland.

Amsterdam in spring?—Truly Shitsville. Pot fumes wafting out of coffeehouse doorways and horseflies turd-bombing canals.

I checked into my hotel and curtain-wrapped my room. I wanted to call Helen and commune with the airplane woman and Anne Sofie. I felt a jumbo zit on my back. I pulled off my shirt and prepared to pop it in front of the mirror. I noticed a big black mole starting to pulse and seep.

Stop now. Pray. You have your work and God's work to do. Call Helen. Conjure Anne Sofie and the airplane woman. Monitor the mole and suppress its growth mentally.

I did it. I did not second-guess the madness. I eyeballed the mole in mirrors from 30 to 60 times each day. My will interdicted the malignant cells. I believed it. Helen was meeting me in New York City. Publishers were lining up for her book. She knew my body intimately. She would view the mole and determine its status. Her informed opinion would determine a treatment plan.

Prognosis upcoming. Holland, Spain and Great Britain first.

I got through it. I got through it in stunning form—on no sleep, blip sleep and mini-comas, twilight-twined. I was always scared. I willed myself to out-endure a lunacy entirely self-created. I utilized prayer and the native strength of Helen Knode. I employed a mezzo-soprano whom I had never met and a plain-featured woman I'd seen on an airplane. I found a new cavalcade of faces to hold me upright for the moments I glimpsed them and keep my implosion at bay.

Glimpses. Shutter-stop moments. Faces half-hidden by signboards and lost in blinks.

Amsterdam, Barcelona, Madrid. London, the British hinterlands, London again.

It was getting worse. Free fall veered into plummet. My smash book and jaw-dropping mixed reviews meant nothing to me.

But They were always there. And They never caught me looking at Them and never felt endangered under my gaze. There was something sure and kind about each and every one of Them. They all embodied goodness and rectitude.

They all imparted insight and courage, within a rain-drop's span. I swear this is true.

11

Helen viewed the mole and pronounced it benign. I believed her.

It looks the same as it always has. Big Dog, you've been imagining things.

The Intercontinental Hotel, New York City. Two-day rest stop. 31 cities to go.

Helen killed the mole fixation. My anxiety *increased*. I was wired for movement, performance and fantasy. My wife and a hotel room? I don't know what to do.

The first U.S. reviews were out. All praise was undercut with caveats. The book was difficult and intimidating. It was an impressive, but bullying work of art.

I would have preferred fawning magnanimity. The assessment I got?—satisfactory. The bully in me dug it. The book was moving hotcake-fast. Helen took off to meet with *her* potential publishers. My rest stop was all deep breaths and head trips. I went back on the road.

It got worse.

I didn't *look* bad. The tall and gaunt thing has always worked for me. My internal clock was de-sprung, re-sprung and un-sprung. My brain stuttered, sputtered, sparked and always caught ignition. The cities blurred by.

I kept looking in my mouth. I saw bumps and tooth-scrape marks and anointed them cancer. My tongue played over saliva cysts and *made* them metastasize. I ran to mirrors and checked my mouth 50 times a day.

Cities swerved by. I fell into a fugue state. The book went on the *New York Times* best-seller list. The critical consensus held firm as megalomania. My pass-out sleep was worse than no sleep. The bed fell out from under me and took the world with it. I looked at women on airplanes and had sobbing fits. People started looking at me.

I did bookstore events every night. I performed introductory shtick, read from my novel and took questions. I was electrifyingly good in the middle of a meltdown. I always played to one woman in the audience.

I made it to Toronto. The book stayed on the list. Women caught me staring at them and looked away. It horrified me. I willed my eyes elsewhere. The effort made me light-headed. I lost track of where I was.

Evil lad. You always thought you never hurt them. Now they see you.

I got to Chicago. The tour was halfway done. I went to dinner with colleagues and walked to the can. The walls tumbled and compressed. I retained my balance and walked toward a restaurant in Toronto.

It wasn't there. I ran outside and recognized Chicago. I ran back inside and found my colleagues.

It got worse. The cancer-cell migration moved through my mouth. I made it to Milwaukee. I weaved into an elevator at the Pfister Hotel. Three very tall black men evil-eyed me. I weaved and mimicked them.

I made it to the penthouse floor, intact. Reporters were waiting there. I thought they were Ellroy fans. I was wrong. Basketball play-offs were raging. The black guys were Milwaukee Bucks.

The Presidential Suite. Mine for one night. History was

my oyster. The JFK that my characters killed had shacked up right here.

Brutha, you de Man.

I walked through the suite. Fuck, it was huge. The floor rolled. I walked into the world's largest gilt and marble bathroom and walked back out.

The world flew off its axis. Lights throbbed and dimmed as I collapsed in slow motion and hit a silk-brocade bed.

Home.

Kansas City in a heat wave that I knew would never stop.

I bailed on the tour. I knew I'd go insane if I stayed out. My upcoming gigs were canceled. I checked into my Hancock Parkesque manse and shut the world out.

Helen was all love. She knew that the bailout was imperative and praised my persistence up to that point. The diffident Dudley knew that something was wrong and stuck close to his negligent dad.

I surrendered. I thought I'd crash in exultant relief and gain the peace born of a prudent relinquishment. I was mistaken. It just got worse.

I couldn't sleep. I couldn't capitulate to sleep. I thought I'd go into seizures and fall out a window. I thought I'd shoot myself in my sleep. I tossed all the ammunition for the guns in the house and still held on to the fear. I examined my shit for signs of occult blood. I got a knife, pierced a bump on my arm and squeezed cancer cells out. I blackout-curtained my office, sat there and sobbed. I was afraid to think of women. I knew that Helen could read my mind and decode my evil thoughts.

I stayed in the house. I froze out the heat and draped out the light. I walked from room to room, jittered and stuporous. Jaunts outside tore me up. I saw children with their toys and pets and started weeping. All my compartments had crumbled. Everything I'd pushed out rushed straight in. I was 53 years old. It was the sum total of a life lived at warp speed.

Helen looked after me and urged me to get help. Rage played counterpoint to her solicitude. I ran from the marriage. I ran straight into a crack-up. She'd just landed a sweet two-book deal with a prestige publisher. She did not believe that it brought me great joy and that I was moved by her conquest of a very difficult craft. I had devolved from flesh and blood lover to sanitarium guest. She went from lover to crazy man's nurse and stood before me, depleted and furious.

She shamed me into seeking help. I did restorative yoga and got acupuncture. I got zero-balance massage and shiatsu massage. It didn't do shit. I went to a swami's health retreat in rural Iowa. I got slathered with healing oils and learned transcendental meditation. It didn't do shit. I saw a medical doctor, got a complete checkup and learned that I was in fine health. The doctor prescribed anti-depressant pills. They did not chill my anxiety or calm my nerves. They enhanced my libido as they shriveled my dick. I drove around K.C., staring at women. I visited my Anne Sofie von Otter poster, stashed up in the attic. I looked at it and cried.

I sat in dark rooms. The Kansas City summer blazed. Helen played nursemaid and Dudley ignored me. The doctor prescribed sedatives and sleeping pills. I resisted them, succumbed to them and slowly became addicted.

I sought oblivion the way I had once sought stratospheric stimulation. I assaulted my sleep deficit and tried to halt my fifty-year sprint. The sleeping pills knocked me out. They did not provide me with serenity upon awakening. The sedatives slightly re-plugged my voltage and let me walk the world sans tremors and tears.

Helen and I built separate compartments and slept in

separate beds. The dog sided with her. I put the new novel on hold. I wrote movies and TV shows and earned good dough. I never wrote under the influence. The challenge of constructing narrative sustained me. My paid-work narrative paled beside my internal monologues.

They were wholly about WOMEN. They were about WOMEN and nothing else.

They featured Anne Sofie von Otter and the airplane woman. They featured the wish-named Joan appropriately aged and the real Joan foretold and misunderstood. I employed the same story line with all of the women. It was the tale of Helen Knode and me—but this time I did not fuck it up.

We moved to the mid-California coast. It was summer '02. We dumped the swank K.C. pad for a profit and brought a swank Carmel pad. Helen did all the relocation work. It infuriated her. I was zoned out, sleeping or working. I was out staring at women or off on some loony love trip in my head.

We still held out hope for the marriage. I concealed the extent of my addiction and talked a good game of change. Helen was indefatigably optimistic. It was, and is, a hallmark of her warrior's soul.

She didn't know how badly I was strung out. She had always known me as a man indeterminately off in his head.

It got worse.

I cut down to L.A. for film-script meetings. I extended the trips to hole up at the Beverly Wilshire Hotel. I popped herbal uppers from a health-food store. I explored my newfound passion for a dead poetess.

Anne Sexton: 1928–'74. Pillhead, profligate soul, neurasthenic icon. Dead at 45: self-inflicted carbon monoxide.

Paperback covers. The woman with her knees against a swimming-pool ledge. The woman in a summer shift dress.

Mother, I will never relinquish you. Mother, I will always seek your emblem. At least The Curse I inflicted on you gave me that.

Priapic rites in a dark room. Two frayed book covers. One floor lamp to light my watcher's path.

It got worse. I slammed myself between sleep comas and ecstatic imagery. Helen and I pulled further apart. She realized the force of my secret inner life and grew astonished and then appalled. I overdosed and woke up in a Monterey nut ward. Helen bailed me out. I fled to a health farm in Arizona. I overdosed and woke up in a Tucson nut ward. Helen bailed me out. We returned to Carmel. I OD'd again. Helen demanded that I clean up now and forever. I entered a thirty-day program and did just that.

It got worse.

Because my options had run out.

Because there was no place to run *to*.

Because Helen Knode was all indictment.

Early fall '03. That plush house and coastal rainstorms.

Nothing clicked inside me. Nothing felt right. All my apologies felt hollow. All my vows to change trailed out half-spoken and dead.

I didn't know what to do next. It was the first time in my life that had happened.

We'd danced around it before. It was always abstract. A permissive '70s concept. Repellent and seductive and ever euphemistic: a relaxed civil contract.

We were sitting in the kitchen. Helen gave it a quivery real voice.

Stay married/other people/be dignified and proper/ "Don't ask, don't tell."

Of course, I agreed.

It was an opportunity.

Now I know what to do next.

PART IV

GODDESS

She kissed me at Coit Tower. San Francisco was summer cold. I underdressed for the walk and didn't factor in high monuments and wind. The sun was up, the view was wide, tourists clucked and snapped photographs. I shivered. She rubbed my arms warm.

Joan. The prophecy revealed. The real her, 46 years later.

The kiss stunned me. I'd brain-scheduled it for the hotel later. Coit Tower rolled.

My nerves still were shot. I was seven months into my Helen deal and nine months dope-free. Joan had rough hands and a tendency to stride ahead of me. I walked faster. She noticed that it was rude and held my arm to correct her pace.

The kiss worked. A sun blast quashed my shivers. We found the fit and hit the right note of decorum. We disengaged simultaneous. Joan smiled to acknowledge it. She asked me if I was okay. I said, What do you mean? She said, It's your eyes. You can't tell if you're angry or hurt.

She was 38. Her gray hair and my smooth features subverted the age gap. My post-crack-up world looked garish. I was always tensed up to fight or run.

We walked down Telegraph Hill. The short steps messed with my long legs. Joan steadied me.

We knew our assignments already. We misread the cost at the start. My job was to fall. Her job was to catch me on the way down.

12

Helen hated me.

She suppressed it through my crack-up. I ran from the marriage and bled her solicitude dry. I slept and brooded my way through the move west. Helen again did the shit work. I voyeur-perved women and full-time fantasized. Dudley died of a heart attack. Helen held a candlelight vigil and bid his soul heaven-bound. I ran from the sight of our beloved dog dead and passed out.

Her fury was always checked by her love for me. I depleted her stores of goodwill and left her shell-shocked. My always-present self-absorption veered to vacancy. My insanity pushed Helen to a crazed psychic state. She watched her brilliant husband squander his internal solvency. She put her career on hold to play wet nurse. Our new house symbolized the worst of it.

A beautiful thatched cottage in the Carmel hills. Allegedly Clark Gable's ex-pad. A big price tag. Big upgrade expenses. A dream home–cum–life raft.

I was drowning. Helen was sternly afloat. I ignored the lines she tossed me. I tried to push her head under the water. I did not know it at the time.

Nest, haven, safety zone. A road flare to mark resurrection.

Helen marshaled artisans and workmen. Two-story beams were glazed and re-set. A river-rock fireplace was laid in, stone by stone. The kitchen featured a half-ton marble island. The master bedroom offered an ocean view. My office was two stories high and built on three levels. My desk was presidential-size. The walls were festooned with framed book jackets and award scrolls.

I earned the money that paid for it. I did nothing else.

I was checked out, AWOL, gone fishin'. Helen watched our bank balance evaporate. I popped uppers and downers. I eyeballed women at shopping malls. I stared at pictures of Anne Sexton and interdicted her suicide.

Jean Hilliker would have been 88 on our housewarming date. The Hilliker Curse was 45 years old. I did not acknowledge it then.

Sobriety was no cure-all. I glibly assumed it would be. We didn't go broke. I pulled myself out of the shit again. God had more to do with it than I did. I believed it then and believe it more certainly now.

I was frayed, fraught, french-fried and frazzled. I lost a bunch of dope-bloat pounds and started looking good once more. I perched at the door of Whew, we're okay now. Helen would not let me in.

I thought my sober state would cancel all debts and put us ahead of the game. Helen once quoted Clifford Odets and called me "a bullet with nothing but a future." The epigram implied my ability to exploit my own past. I stood ready to resume my life's trajectory. The preceding two and a half years were largely blurry. Fall '03: Helen refills my memory bank.

You drove around Carmel in shit-stained trousers. My friends heard you jacking off upstairs. You were vile to my family. You peeped women while you walked Dudley. You went to a network pitch meeting, bombed. You'd dribbled ice cream on your shirt. An executive asked you to describe your TV pilot. You said it was about cops rousting fags and jigs. You ran your car off the 101 and came home bloody. You got four speeding tickets and jacked up our insurance to ten grand a year. You were cavalier and oblivious while I forfeited my career momentum to save you from yourself. You became someone else as I watched helplessly and came to hate myself and doubt my own sanity for having stayed with you.

My riposte was, I never cheated on you. Helen's riposte was, It doesn't matter—it's all in your head anyway.

Fall '03. The dream house and coastal rainstorms. Helen's hurt and rage. Helen's open-union offer. My antennae twitching—no, not just yet.

We got a new bull terrier and named her Margaret. She instantly swooned for Helen and evinced outrage for me. Margaret followed me through the pad, barking and growling. Margaret's outrage remains, to this day.

I couldn't get past Helen's grief. I couldn't repent or atone. My old shtick crashed and burned. Helen rebuffed my vows with shrugs. I drove around Carmel and blasted Beethoven. I sat in espresso joints and watched women. I hurled myself at my office couch every night. I prayed for Helen and Margaret and asked God for signs. I crammed myself into plush upholstery and tried to will sleep.

'03 into '04. The dream house, the separate lives, the feminist/separatist hound.

I wrote three novellas to fill out a collection. They were sadly comedic. They detailed a fucked-up cop in love with a big-time actress. The cop narrated the stories from heaven. He was waiting for the woman, but he didn't want her to die.

The big cosmic joke. My life's trajectory, retold for laffs.

I always get what I want. It comes slow or fast and always costs a great deal. I have honed the conjurer's art with an astonishingly single-minded precision.

A friend asked me to give a speech at Cal Davis. I knew She'd be there.

I said, "You remind me of someone."

She said, "Tell me about her."

"I never spoke to her."

"Why?"

"I was afraid to."

"Why?"

"I was a child. I was ashamed of the thoughts I'd been having."

"What was she like?"

"She was a fine person."

"How do you know that, if you never spoke to her?"

"I spent a lot of time watching her."

"Was that a common childhood practice of yours?"

"Yes."

"And it remains one?"

"Yes."

"What was the girl's name?"

"I don't know, but I named her Joan."

13

The lectern was raised, the room was packed, I had a slay-the-audience view. She sat at the left rear. I caught her gray-streaked hair first. She expanded and filled my frame. Two hundred people receded.

I read from *My Dark Places*. I brain-spoke to the woman at pause points. I described the wish-named Joan and stated the resemblance. The woman was skeptical—college prof up for a fight.

May 28, '04. Sacramento in a spring heat wave. The six thousandth public performance of my dead-mother act.

I was boffo. I read from pitch-perfect memory and laid down even eye contact. I had a pulpit and an eons-deep Protestant bloodline. I was the predatory preacher prowling for prey. The woman was my pivot point. I eyeball-tracked the audience and clicked back to her. She had deep brown eyes. Her features were the wish-named Joan's, aged and age-askewed. I pondered a family resemblance. The woman laughed. It made me toss the thought.

A Q&A session followed. Two hundred sociologists—a dead-mom-tour first. A man asked me how I stage-managed grief.

I cited repetition. I cited faith and a buoyant will that sometimes swerved to obsessiveness. The man called me glib. I brusquely rebuked him. I said she was my mother—not his. I said I'd paid the price—and he hadn't.

The exchange sparked a rumble. I eyeball-drilled the man. He shrugged and shut up. I looked directly at the woman. She looked directly back. She asked me what different forms my mother assumed.

I swooned a little. In that moment, I *knew.*

I pointed to heaven and back down to earth. I said, She's there and I'm here. I said other women had been known to intercede and fuck with my head.

The woman laughed. A few chuckles drifted out. I ended the gig with an elegiac quote. The folks clapped and lined up to get their books signed.

The woman stood behind them and moved toward me in small steps. She got closer and eclipsed the prophecy. Her features became hers alone. She distorted then and now and blitzed iconography. I thanked her for her question and asked her her name.

She said, Joan, and stated her surname. My legs shook. I asked her if she'd like to have a drink later. She said, Assuredly, yes.

Sacramento was the first Joan Zone. It was three hours northeast of Carmel and always swamp hot. It was full of pols and lobbyists sucking the state-government tit. There were hayseed and rock-and-roll contingents. Sacramento always vexed me. That first night was a ghoul show. I got to the lobby bar early. People booze-effused and walked through with cocktails. They were dog-den crashers. I was tensed up to fight or run. First-date portent: I must contain Joan within a public place.

. . .

She showed on time. She'd changed clothes: summer dress to skirt/boots ensemble. Her arms were bare. She had a tattoo on her right bicep. First-date apostasy: I fucking *dug* it.

We arranged chairs beside a table. It was semi-private. I guzzled coffee as Joan sipped scotch. She left lipstick prints on her tumbler. It should have instilled a preacher's kid fury. It didn't. First-date apostasy #2.

She'd read my books and knew some of my story. I supplanted it and laid in a first-date rationale. My wife and I were headed for Splitsville. Divorce was a fait accompli. It was set for an indeterminate date. Helen and I had our deal in the meantime.

I was disingenuous, verging on mendacious. My relationship with Helen was tortuous and open-ended. My life was a daily process of atonement. I could not conceive of a life without Helen Knode. I started double-dealing Joan at the outset. I wanted Helen for companionship and the long shot of sex resurrected. I wanted Joan for her flaming expression of selfhood.

We talked. I got Joan a second scotch. She barely touched it. Not a juicehead—good.

Monologues followed. Joan went first. She was from New York City. Her bloodline was left-wing/Jewish. Mom and dad were divorced. Dad was a college professor and mom was a shrink. She'd been partially raised in a commune. She had a brother in San Francisco. She'd matriculated at Cornell—Helen's alma mater. She had two master's degrees. She was teaching at Cal Davis and was earning her doctorate.

She'd knocked around a lot. She'd pitched some left-wing woo-woo. She'd spent time in the radical women's movement and the punk-rock scene.

I asked her what *punk rock* meant—that shit had slid by

me. Joan called it a rebuttal to Ronald Reagan. I said that I disliked rock and roll and greatly admired Reagan.

It was a test. Joan more than passed it. She smiled and said, That's okay. She picked up my left hand and dropped it in her lap. She laced up our fingers and contained *me*.

I wondered how we looked together. The age/style gap scorched me. I was bald and a foot taller. I felt awkward. I wore a pink polo shirt and wheat jeans.

My monologue followed. I mentioned the crack-up and fresh sobriety. Joan bluntly stated that open-union deals don't work—she'd been through it.

Her jaw was wide. Her mouth connoted harshness and determination. Her smile undermined a seething grievance. A raucous-kid aspect simmered. She knew when to deploy it. She inhabited moments intensely and performed and observed them in concurrence. She was the most stunning woman I had ever seen.

I moved my hand to her knee. I floated someplace. We exchanged phone numbers and addresses. We had some silent spells.

I thanked God for bringing Joan to me. I counted the runs in her black stockings.

The ride home was swervy. I drove too fast and played Beethoven in murmurs and crescendos. I sent Joan flowers and a note en route.

Boomerang car: I zoomed south and whooshed north with equal force.

Helen was out. Margaret growled and retreated to Helen's bedroom. I checked my office phone machine. Joan's name was on the display.

Her message began, "Hey, it's Joan." She continued and thanked me for the flowers. Her voice was softer than it had been the night before. I caught some Brooklyn in her vowels. A few upward tones implied gratitude. She invited me to call her.

I played the message 30-odd times. I memorized every word and every inflection. I don't know how long I cried. It was bright daylight when I started and full night when I stopped.

The Joan Zone, the Knode Abode, three hours between sites. The civil contract that made it okay.

It began with phone calls and letters. The house was large and permitted privacy. I snagged the mail every day. My office was sealed off. Helen rarely walked through. Margaret *stormed* through and barked her outrage. I conducted the courtship sans disruption and overt lies.

It felt exhilarating and wrong. It was a second-to-second Joan-to-Helen parlay. I wanted to regain Helen's respect. I wanted to know who Joan was and what she portended. Joan was new and I was a seasoned opportunist. Opportunists ruthlessly cling to emergent imagery and people. Joan was urgently vivid. My loyalty tipped *toward* her. It made me queasy, despite the deal. I fawned around the dream house in redress. Helen acknowledged my efforts with an offhandedness shaped by her justified grudge. *I wasn't who I said I was.* I sensed that I could never regain my stature.

Opportunists move on. My task was to create credibility with Joan. Written words and phone calls were my métier once more. Joan became the ultimate female spirit in possession of my time alone in the dark.

Her letters were brief. They expressed her attraction to me and ridiculed the Knode-Ellroy contract. My letters described the forthcoming dissolution of the marriage. It was preposterous. I had spent a total of two hours in Joan's presence. I was having it both ways. I was mending fences I intended to jump. Two women got the Ellroy troika: seduce, apologize and explain.

My letters were romantic and oozed sweet intent. I FedExed them to goose the process. I was hard-selling a potential lover. I came on too strong. Joan scolded me and prompted epistolary retreat. I plumbed Joan's character and besieged her with perceptions. I never mentioned her wish-named antecedent. Joan praised my ardor and conceded my acuity. She kept postponing rendezvous in Sacramento and Frisco. I was a dipshit bubblegummer scaling The Mountain of *Looooove*.

It was a tough climb. Joan was a tough woman. I struggled for handholds as she pried at my grip. It was exhilarating. Joan made me work. Written praise sent me summit-bound. Written rebuke kicked me back to earth. I *lived* for her voice in the dark.

Helen and Margaret retired early. My nerves were still shot. Sleep came late, if at all. Panic attacks *still* zapped me daily. Joan and I talked most nights. Her implied rule was, I'll call when I call. I was breathless with the forfeit of male control and mindful of it as a means of seduction. I doused the lights at 9:00 p.m. I played the Chopin nocturnes and killed the sound at 9:45. Darkness held me. I heard crickets and the waves on Carmel beach. The phone rang when it rang—and almost always at 10:30.

She always said, "Hey, it's Joan." Her voice carried a husk and registered as mid-range contralto. I'd ask her if her hair was up or down and whether or not she was wearing her glasses. She'd say "Up" or "Down" and "Yes" or "No" with a swoopy inflection. It always pulled tears out of me. I never told her this. I was grateful for every small kindness she showed me. My gratitude was there at the start. My gratitude remains in Joan's long-standing absence.

Our talks were affectionate and often contentious. Joan's university status bewildered me. I didn't quite get what she did. She provided brisk word portraits of her many friends and colleagues. My interest waned then. I wanted to milk our sex vibe and set up a face-to-face meet. Academic code deterred me. I believed that anecdotes should ping-pong between people. Joan questioned my interlocutory style. I was supposed to respond along set lines and not talk about myself so much. Academians deployed this method and balked when interlocutors ignored it. This constrained me. I wanted to wow Joan with my story. She wanted to establish parity with a storytelling pro. I came up short most times. I was bucking a woman from a different world and another generation. Our talks always got around to *us* at the phone-call finale. The road ran circuitous. Joan challenged me. I found a way to stay in the fight. I knew that I had to change. My old woman ways had decimated my marriage. Joan astounded me. I had to think and act from her perspective. It felt like film noir. The amnesiac assumes that the black-clad woman has the answers. The price was a certain submission. It rankled me. I respected Joan for her fight. I wanted to get her to an enclosed space. I wanted to tussle with her and get past words. I believed that mutual surrender would lead us someplace very *soft*.

She was left-wing, I was right-wing. She was Jewish, I was Gentile. She was an atheist, I was a believer. Her cultural influences bored me. Her punk-rock shit was jejune. Our conversations fractured and rebuilt around desire. We flabbergasted each other. She possessed a surpassing personal power. I told her this. Joan told me that my power leveled her. She hinted at a roundelay of role reversals. We always got there as we said good night. I always put the phone down, trembling.

. . .

I won a book prize in Italy. It entailed an a.m. flight from Frisco. I decided to spend the preceding night there. Joan agreed to meet me.

I got a suite at the Ritz-Carlton. Joan rang the bell right on time. I held her in the doorway. She found the suite constraining and suggested a stroll. Her local travelogue delighted me. The Coit Tower kiss kept me attentive. I let her walk ahead of me. She saw it as packed-street etiquette and my means to study her. She let me take charge then. I took her hand and spieled a run of kid-crime tales. She laughed and let me lead her to a restaurant. I didn't want to eat and blitz my adrenaline rush. She understood. She studied me and reported her findings.

She nailed my beady eyes. They were ruthless. My body language was jerky *and* deferential. That showed my desire and my instinct not to crowd her. I riffed on her performing sense and her tripartite inhabiting of all moments. She said I was the first man who ever got that.

We walked uphill to the Ritz. Our legs fluttered. We kissed until 3:00 a.m. and kept our clothes on. I pre-imagined one thing correctly. The clash was strenuous. Our bodies ached from the meld.

Milan was a portable Joan Zone. Our transatlantic calls featured a softened rapport and frequent sex sighs. Carmel was Joan and Helen coiled contrapuntal. My moral sanction impeded, rather than liberated, me. I felt loyal to both women. I had to regain Helen's trust and gain Joan's trust. The deal was "Don't ask/Don't tell." Helen did not say "Don't pray" and "Don't brood." The Hilliker Curse required me to protect *all* the women I loved. There were two of them now. Prayer pushed me toward either/or dictums. I was, and am, decisive by nature. That native trait failed me here. Extra brood sessions compensated. I assessed Helen and Joan sans a decision-making process. I came to this: they were the only two women who had ever astonished me.

They emboldened me and made me fear my heedless maleness. They encompassed differing strains of strongly held belief and made me ponder meaning. Helen's swami shtick imbued my Christian view with a lighter secular touch. Joan's strident leftism gave me the passion of the red flag aswirl and contextualized her personal grievance as historical and therefore empirically valid. They were big women suffused with big ideas. Helen and I had 13 years together. She still had the power to move me, jazz me, fuel me. I had squandered sex with her. It felt irretrievable. Joan was the prospect of sex as endless ride. Joan represented dialogue to spark enormous change. Her sporadic softness engendered my full-time softness. All my praying and brooding buttressed my love for both women. My addiction to woman imagery and the force of The Curse pushed me toward Joan.

Summer courtship, '04. The prelude extends.

Joan invited me to Sacto for Independence Day. It's a long weekend. Get a room at the Sheraton—it's near my place.

A film-director colleague lived close by. That provided my alibi. I drove up in an ever-present heat wave. The Delta Valley was always hot. This was the blast oven–Everglades combo. I checked in at the hotel and walked to Joan's pad with flowers.

She wore a white blouse and jeans. Her hair was down and she wore her glasses. I smiled at that. Joan said "Down" and "Yes" and kissed my cheek. She put the flowers in a vase. I checked out her bookshelves. The only shit I recognized were three of my own novels. The other tomes: labor history, Commie tracts, gender polemics.

Window units barely kept the heat out. Sweat seeped through my shirt. My pulse raced and produced more wetness. Joan served a roast chicken and salad dinner. It was simple and tasty. I hardly touched it. Talk was difficult. I wanted to tell her everything I'd never revealed to a woman. Helen trumped Joan here. She already knew *all* my stories. Joan chatted up her teaching load and a bar-b-q the next day. Some friends were throwing a bash. I was invited.

All I had were expressions of love and alone-in-the-dark perceptions. They seemed precipitous and untimely. Declarations of chivalry bubbled up and almost choked out. Joan mentioned her atheism. My chivalry pitch cited God as a primary resource. I kept my mouth shut. I got tensed up to fight or run.

We washed the dishes and sat down on the couch. Joan smiled. Some lipstick was stuck to her teeth. I wiped it off with my shirttail. Joan asked me what I was afraid of. I said, "You." I asked her what she was afraid of. She pointed to me.

We kissed. We fell into the meld and stayed there. Joan held my face. I kissed her gray streaks. Joan pushed the coffee table back to make room for my legs.

I started to lay out my declarations. Joan touched my lips and shushed me. My heart rate went haywire. Joan sensed something wrong and held me. My shirt was halfway off. Joan removed it. I unbuttoned her blouse. I saw her breasts and started sobbing.

She let it be for a while. She said things like "Hey, now." She saw that it wasn't about to stop. She eased me up and got me to the door and told me she'd see me tomorrow.

. . .

Sleep was impossible. The air conditioner rattled and tossed ice chips. Drunks careened down the outside hallway all night.

I kept the lights off. I saw Joan's face and fought half-nude imagery. I conjured Helen and told her we could work things out. I never completed my spiels. Joan appeared, Joan smiled, I dabbed traces of red off her teeth.

The bar-b-q was above Sacramento, near the UC campus. Joan had a VW stamped with pro-labor stickers. We crossed a drawbridge and hit a greenbelt. Joan said, Last night was all right, you know. I touched her hand on the steering wheel. She curled a finger around my wrist.

We drove in silence. It marked fifty rides we took in a similar quiet. I never knew what Joan was thinking. I would have given anything to know then. I would give anything to know now.

The shindig was outdoors. The crowd was thirtyish academics. Joan introduced me around. She kept a hand on my arm to indicate that we were a couple. It was stunningly decorous. She said "James" and left off the Ellroy. I felt weightless without my hot-shit surname. Joan caught it and touched me that much more.

Sunstroke heat, burgers and guacamole. Weightlessness and sleeplessness. The vertigo that Joan always inspired.

A young couple recognized me. That gave me a task beyond yearn and obsess. I regaled them with outtakes from my perved-out past. I eyeball-trolled for Joan about once per minute. I caught her looking my way at the same rate. She winked on one occasion.

. . .

My hotel was near the statehouse. We watched a fireworks display from my room.

Joan sat on the window ledge. I sat on the bed. We imbibed room-service libations. The show produced a sputtery sound track. Joan's silence was a roar. I started to tell a trademark story. Joan said, "I've read your books, you know."

The fireworks crescendoed and died. I smelled gunpowder through the AC vents. Joan walked to the door. I got up and followed her. She touched my cheek and told me not to worry.

Sleep was impossible. I was terrified. She walked out the door and took my body with her. I checked my mouth for malignant bumps and my arms for seeping melanomas. I went from the bed to the bathroom mirror, all night. I conjured Joan's face. The process tore at my fear. Every Joan image invoked Helen. Every Helen image returned me to Joan.

Dawn came up. I forced myself to shave and shower. I bolted half a bagel and coffee. I was tensed up to fight or run. There was no one to fight. I had no body to fight with—so I ran.

I drove to Joan's place and rang the bell. Joan opened up and saw me. She sat me down and let me find some breath. I got light-headed words out. "I love you," "I'm scared," and "I've got to go home" are all I remember.

The dream house was empty. Margaret was kenneled up. Helen was back in K.C. with her mother. I gobbled food out of the refrigerator and fell down on the couch. I woke up at midnight. I ran to my phone machine. The number 0 glowed.

Four days went by. I called Helen in K.C. and reveled in her family minutiae. I worked on a TV pilot and played raging Beethoven and soft Rachmaninoff. I wondered when I'd get my body back. I saw her face every few seconds. It wasn't a conjuring. She was omniscient.

The doorbell rang. Friday, midafternoon, FedEx for sure.

Take note of what you are seeking, for it is—

She looked grave and sweet, all bollixed some new way. She said, "Hi," with her swoopy inflection.

I folded her up and kissed her gray streaks. I said, "I'll never run away again."

14

But I did.

But not far.

But not for long.

I was the amnesiac. She was the black-clad woman with the answers.

Joan raided my image bank. It was a yippie prank. The Red Goddess decreed that all women should look like her and that I should seek only her revised portrait. She gave herself to me and eluded me. She gave me the knowledge that all women *were* her and that any terrified exits were just preludes to runs back.

No faces looked like Her. No new images replaced Her. Every partial resemblance dispersed into pixilated dots. No woman could ever be Her. No face read for the power to redeem could ever connote what She gave me and what She withheld. I stopped looking. There was Her and nobody else.

Goddess: Beckon me and cast me out. Let me worship and learn, love thee and fear thee. Partake of my reckless spirit and know that I am soul-pure. I am falling. No place is safe. Savagely sanction me to seek the world in Thy name.

My nerves were *still* shot. Sleep remained problematic. I juiced my original cover lie to explain my weekends away. I stayed in the dream house with Helen. Margaret remained outraged. I relinquished myself to romantic fixation and built bridges at home. I was sober, I made money, Helen's anger withered as her grudge snap-crackle-popped. I repented less and brooded more. Helen researched her new novel and made a bevy of friends. I wondered if she sought male action, and decided, *C'est la guerre*. I got smug. We had an agreement. Helen sensed my preoccupation as a return to form. He's back, he's less crazy, he's off—per always—in his head.

Joan. The power of name. Strong-willed lovers Sturm-und-Dranged.

Joan despised my Helen deal. We had no deal ourselves. I refused to ask, Joan refused to grant. Helen and Joan were grudge holders. I was not. I was a movin'-on guy on a two-way track. It was a three-hour drive between women. Joan and I collided most weekends. Our time apart allowed me to yearn and seek Her in prayer.

Yearning is my chief fount of inspiration. I live in that exalted state. The drama of women sought and fleetingly found competes with History as tidal wave. My dark-room communion has given me a world to rewrite. Wanting what I cannot have commands me to create large-scale art in compensation. My broad social arcs backdrop big love at all costs. I must contain these stories and create perfect love in book form. Unfound women counterbalance History as random horror. I must bestow grandeur on my mother's death and err on empathy's side with all my depictions of women. The Hilliker Curse was a self-inflicted summons to compulsion and predation. The Hilliker Curse charged me to sit in the dark and seek art. The Red Goddess Joan obliterated other women for me. She left me gasping for meaning. I began to see her *as* History.

Our time apart was my monk's retreat, shot through

with phone sex. Our time together was a passion play with an often dissonant chorus.

Joan took me everywhere. Sex was an unending surprise and an ever-replenishing joy. Talk was bewilderment, enlightenment and vexation. My theme was, you must change me and I must protect you. It was highly specious and unassailably tender. It allowed me to hear shit that I didn't want to hear and stay in the war.

Joan's atheism killed me. I eschewed Christian text and laid on a soupçon of deistic jive. I *listened*. My code was, Tolerance does not equal approval and should not be construed as censure. Joan's leftist/anarchist shit bugged me. I *listened*. I conformed to her interlocutory style and asked gee whiz–phrased questions. I fucking *tried*. Joan loved me for it. I loved her for loving me. Every acknowledgment of my flowering heart gut-shot me with gratitude. We told each other sex stories. Joan chortled at my previous exploits. I portrayed them as buffoonish, to spare her pain and allay jealousy. We did not achieve parity here. Joan described good pre-Ellroy sex in wild-ass detail. It titillated me, horrified me, enraged me and moved me. The black-clad woman has the answers. She is your seditious sister. The easy answer is, She is you and you are She. The Christian answer is, Judge not, lest ye be judged. The hard answer is, Acceptance means loss of control.

We diverged and reconnected along odd lines. Our social codes dovetailed unexpectedly. I was a door-holder and a ladies-firster. Joan dug that. I never scoped other women in her presence. Joan *loooooooved* that. Her brazen brother was a fascist, a religionist, a heterosexist. It didn't matter. He was a good human being, and he was sweet to her.

She cut me open. I lived for her approval and wept at her harshness. I left blood spills wherever we went.

Our love was immediate and unimpinged by commitment. My relationship with Helen killed the chance of a sanctified US. *I* was at fault here, *I* was confused, *I* was atypically risk-averse. Joan weathered this with grace and very few expressions of displeasure. She let me stay in the fight. I was *always* tensed up to fight or run. We fought. I ceded control in reluctant increments. Joan noted my efforts and gave me no reason to run.

I found the reasons, alone in the dark.

Sacramento to Carmel. The Joan Zone to the dream house, bereft. The Red Goddess to the best friend/roommate and her outraged dog.

The Hilliker Curse. Bylaw #1: You must protect *all* the women you love.

Helen never questioned my time away and always welcomed me back. I left my body and my design for conquest and surrender three hours northeast. I returned to Helen in all her goodness and unique brilliance. She'd softened toward me. I assumed the role of companion-husband sans bedroom access. I crashed—just a little. The roar of Joan subsided—just a *touch*.

The phone rang every other night. Anticipation kept me breathless. I felt unbodied. My need and taste for acquiescence horrified me. I fixated on Joan's past. I feared her susceptibility. My sex tales stressed pathos. Her sex tales stressed seXXX. My fear stretched to encompass our inimical worldviews. I had become a sponge for reassurance and consolation. It appalled me. My need for titillation felt masochistic. It registered as peeping turned inside out.

I brooded. I prayed. I toured for my journalistic collection. I called Joan from dark hotel rooms in a dozen cities. A new book and new acclaim. It felt like my old and safe world, redux.

Joan and I were six months in. I knew the sex would

never diminish and the roar would never abate. I couldn't grapple the walls between us. A sob at the top of my chest was permanently stuck. I felt unreasonable. I felt infantile. I wanted more, more and more. It was staggeringly MORE than any sane woman could give.

I flew to a Mexican book fair. I told Joan I'd call en route. I didn't. I felt unequal to her weight. I felt soul-frail. I abdicated. I vowed survival in apostasy's name.

Misalliance, folie à deux, obsession. I mistakenly defined us as that.

She said, "You look the same."

I said, "So do you."

"It hasn't been that long."

"You haven't asked me for an explanation."

"I don't need one. It got to be too much for you. I would have done the same thing if you hadn't."

"You would have done it more gracefully."

"I'm not sure."

"I am. You were always more gracious than me."

"I was surprised that you didn't return my calls. The phone was always your guiltiest pleasure."

"I didn't want to be tempted. I was afraid I'd go crazy with it all over again."

"That might very well happen."

"I'll risk it."

"You say that now."

"I want to try again."

"Why?"

"There's no one but you."

15

Winter '05 was a dreamscape. Coastal storms indoor-contained me. Joan called twice. I ignored her swoopy inflections and erased the messages. The dream house four-walled the dreamscape. I sat still and brooded up hours. Helen went about her work life and social life. Margaret oppressed me. The Red Goddess appeared at least once per minute. She showed up conjured *and* unbidden. Her ban on images of other women remained in effect. I could think of no one else.

I tried. I screened Marcia Sidwell, the airplane woman, Marge on the train. I was internally resistant. Anne Sofie von Otter and Anne Sexton, ditto. Likewise the woman from that rainy-night dream.

Rain. 1980 to 2005. Joan as childhood imagery transmogrified. The other woman still recalled and real-life unfulfilled.

My image bank remained intact. It stored the monomaniacal overflow of my world-class memory. It was a dormitory full of women the Goddess had slain. I got what I had always *really* wanted. I was alone with one woman who would never reappear and dash her power with the demands of real life.

I was overdue to write a new novel. I was bored with film and TV work. Journalism and short stories were snoresville.

I got a bug up my ass to write GIANT fiction. I had plot points, characters and historical flow brain-prepped. Helen urged me to create a less rigorous style and shape it with greater emotion. The crack-up had deadened my soul. My soul was astir now. I had an armored-car heist, black-militant shit, the late-'60s zeitgeist. I had protagonists, connective tissue, history writ small. I did not have the guts of the novel. A rainy-night brood session provided it.

Joan.

The Red Goddess as the unifying force of four years of History.

Our clash of wills, our war of belief, that woman's immensity exploded and *contained.*

I waited in the dark for the phone to ring. I played the Hammerklavier adagio in summons. I waited three weeks. She didn't call. She sent me a card, instead.

It included birthday wishes and concluded with a poem. It ended with the word "Prayer."

She came that far. She honored our separateness that deeply. She assured my eternal love.

Rain pounded San Francisco. The cab traffic-crawled and contained us. Space constraints and inclination kept us pressed close.

It stayed non-verbal. The cabbie was a witness. He dropped us at a restaurant in Sea· Cliff. The place was crowded and deterred conversation. Small talk got us through dinner and a cab ride to the Fairmont Hotel. My call: drinks at the Tonga Room.

A tiki bar with a barge sunk in chlorinated water. Wall torches and carved god masks. The barge band played oldie covers. We imbibed the usual: scotch and coffee.

Joan was pensive. I was full of grand declaration. Joan's

quiet gaze doused the volume and shut it off. I felt bombastic. I demanded the world in every moment. Joan looked exhausted. I saw what I had cost her so far.

The corny music was a life raft. Our talk floated in sync. We chitchatted, segued into it and got *to* it. There were no interruptions or silent intervals. The All-Souls Retreat meets the Worker's Collective. Commie-cell minutes and Lutheran call-and-response.

My bullshit open marriage, her abrupt moods, our temperaments that no lover had ever withstood. My delusional expectations. Her debilitating brusqueness. Our incomprehensibly different worlds.

My controlling nature. Her controlling nature. Our conflicting surrender pacts. Our amalgam of white and red flags aswirl.

Our big hurt. Our dear love. Our moments of two different worlds subsumed.

We let it trail off. We watched fat tourists dance. Our eyes found each other's. We both nodded yes.

Winter courtship, '05. The process *re*-extends. Chaste weekends in Sacramento. Sex postponed and reinvented. A chastened rapport and a pre-commitment plunge.

I stayed at a hotel near Joan's place. My cover lies became more convoluted. "My colleague" in Sacto—epic falsehood now. Lying killed me. The added mendaciousness made it worse. The re-courtship softened Joan. I started to think marriage, daughter, dog. The jaunts between women sapped me. I wanted to rebuild a dream house in the Red Goddess's name and reconsecrate the sacrament of marriage. Joan was planning a move to San Francisco. I dream-built our love shack by the Bay and reimagined holy matrimony again.

My nerves were *less* than shot. My sleep was *less* problematic. I was *less* inclined to fight or run. The decarnalizing process tempered Joan and de-clawed me. We talked about sex, but didn't do it. Joan reemerged and *re*-stunned me. I got *re*-obsessed within chaste boundaries. I reconceived our life together and repopulated it with ideals.

Paradox, dichotomy, dialectic. The Diaspora meets the Reformation. Our divergent beliefs *contained*. Our corporeal selves reconstituted with a daughter. My safety-zone concept deconstructed with someone dangerous. I was the amnesiac. She was the black-clad woman with the answers.

There was a *single* answer. It was Family. Joan never stated the word as goal or solution and refrained from comments on my familyless state. Jean Hilliker dumped my old man in November '55. I was five decades into my only child/orphan/skirt-chaser/part-time husband act. Joan and I read wrong on paper. I revised our differences to read defiantly right. Prayer brought me to the concept of consolidation. Brood time brought me to a vision of parenthood and the mandate to fight even harder for an even truer cause and perhaps create a plane of unimaginable sanctification.

I told Helen that I'd met a woman. She winced and said, I know. She cried a little. I inquired about *her* action. She laughed and refused to tell.

I continued with TV and film work. I pored through research briefs and compiled a set of notes for my novel. I never told Joan, *This Book Is You*. I wanted to de-bombasticize. I wanted to reseal the union in a clarified state. We were buying time to observe ourselves. We were recycled lovers. I was bopping between dream houses, gone-bust and future. I was ever the amnesiac. I was ever prone to relive the life I forgot.

. . .

Re-consummation was joyful. The six-week prelude ended in Sacto, fresh with spring heat. The victory of resurrection jazzed me. I started predicting our future. Joan withstood a dose of it and blew up.

Not restricted by your marriage, not without more trust of you, not with you on some maniac roll.

I listened. I *heard* the answer. Joan didn't ask me or tell me to bail on the marriage. She told me not to jerk her chain.

Joan always knew how to play me. It wasn't guile. She understood that her best weapon was the truth.

I wanted more and more of her. I wanted honor to reign at our core. I didn't want to cause Helen even more pain. The word *Divorce* ratched me. I wanted it both ways. I tend to err on the side of high cost and risk. I felt it coming here.

Spring into summer. Hotel weekends in San Francisco and dinners with Joan's friends. Late lessons in social etiquette and the merging of lives. Lessons that I learned. Lessons rewarded with Joan's bright eyes and light touch.

I was grateful for every small kindness she showed me. The gratitude was there that second summer. The gratitude remains with Joan gone.

We spent the Fourth of July in Frisco. We had drinks at the Tonga Room and walked back to our hotel. It was downhill. We steadied each other. Joan slid on her slick-soled shoes. I kept an arm around her and swooped her back up. The hotel suite was red-walled and sconce-lit. Joan plugged in a CD player and performed a torrid dance. Her movements were stunning and shocking. Her black garments fell just out of my reach.

Lover, goddess, redeemer. Possessed eyes that went swoopy the instant the music stopped.

. . .

Joan slept. I didn't. The black garments remained on the floor.

Dawn hit early. I cracked the drapes for some light. I circled the bed and watched Joan from different angles. I saw a dozen sides of her with every tuck and stretch.

So be it. Whatever it costs, whatever it takes.

We said good-bye a few hours later. Joan drove home to Sacto and I drove home to Carmel. I told Helen then. We both cried. I fished for reassurance and got it. Yes, it was inevitable. Yes, it has to be. Yes, it's the right thing.

We cut our financial deal there in the kitchen. I was grandiosely generous. I told Helen that I'd always take care of her. She said, I know you will.

We debriefed a fourteen-year marriage. Blame got spread bilaterally. We laughed a little and steered clear of the obvious detours. The talk did not relieve me. I felt shallow and cruel.

Helen had tea. I cued up Joan images and felt my brain screen lurch. I saw Jean Hilliker. I calculated her current age as 90. I recalled March of '58, and the day I inflicted The Curse.

16

Joan was fearful more than moved. She explained why. She rarely knew when I acted from a sense of drama or from a viable truth.

So women will love me. So I get what I want. There is no other truth.

I moved into a nearby Carmel apartment. Helen helped me pack. We put the dream house on the market and retained divorce lawyers. My lawyer found my largesse unnerving and financially unsound. I told her, Tough shit. Helen's lawyer said, I dig this guy. He lets it all hang out.

Joan moved to San Francisco. I helped her pack and unpack boxes and do the shit work. The relocation felt right. Frisco became the new Joan Zone. Carmel was less than two hours south.

We orbited closer. I resisted an impulse to crowd Joan. I wanted to hover near Helen. Fence jumper/fence straddler/fence jumper. Fences and the two women I loved.

The divorce went forward. The house went unsold. Joan and I spent weekends in her town and mine. We enjoyed an idyll in West Marin County. We took walks and made love in a country inn. I described her transit of History in my novel. The wish-named Joan to the real Joan to the fictive Red Goddess named Joan Rosen Klein. Joan said she felt honored. She took my hand and placed it over her heart.

Helen and I moved forward in our own way. We formed a friendship and style pact. We vowed to comport ourselves as the world's grooviest exes. The relationship was frayed raw. Helen dismissed Joan as an older man's folly and damned my bulletproof heart. She never questioned my loyalty. She critiqued my eagerness to live in puerile fixation. She cited a single source: Jean Hilliker.

I had to keep Helen safe. I had to make Joan safe. We started discussing the possibility of a child. We both wanted a daughter. Joan loved the name Ruth. It rolled off the tongue and was resoundingly Jewish. I liked the name. It complemented Ellroy and sealed our Judeo-Christian pact. Joan nixed Ellroy and her own surname. She suggested Hilliker for our daughter.

It was like that. The Red Goddess went that deep. How could it go wrong?

The apartment came furnished and stocked with dishes and towels. It reeked of transience. It vibed fuck pad and divorce stopgap. Joan was 125 miles and a zillion light-years away. Helen was one mile and ten zillion. I settled in. I started to go breathless and squirrelly.

I got a script deal and goosed the Ellroy-Knode bank account. I fretted about Helen. Our years together cut through me and lodged as a sob. I lived for weekends with Joan. I sat in the dark and ached for weekday-night phone calls. The dream house sat on the market. The cash split and alimony contract meant big workloads forever. I creamed for the macho-maimed struggle of it all. My nerves started shearing. My sleep vaporized. Those melanomas kept popping up on my arms. Brain scrolls of Joan wiped the cancer cells out.

Fall '05. The ratchets tighten. I live for the Red Goddess that much more.

We were committed now. I had trashed my life to assure an honorable union. Joan was grateful and perplexed. My burn-the-world-down mentality amazed and terrified her. It bid me to greater expectations and instilled an even greater lust.

Joan swooned and resisted. We had moments of great beauty. She told me the stories she'd withheld and let me hold her, sobbing. She refused to attend a police function honoring me. It entailed the Pledge of Allegiance and socializing with cops.

We spent time in West Marin County. We floated in hot tubs with wide river views. We had an hours-long fight on the subject of graffiti.

My nerves were shot. I got tensed up to fight or run. I lived for that much more of her.

I gave a reading performance in L.A. Big stage, packed house. I read a twenty-minute monologue and nailed it to the stars. Big applause erupted. I blew Joan a kiss. All eyes were on me—except hers. I hobnobbed with the audience after the show. A tall woman approached me. She was strong-featured and wore crooked glasses. Her hair was not quite blond and not quite red. We talked. She came forward in laughter and nearly gasped in retreat. She was the woman from my 1980 rainy-night dream.

Joan hovered. I never got the woman's name. Joan and I walked to my car. I thought of Marcia Sidwell out of nowhere.

I willed the dream woman away. She recurred sporadically, in new dreams. I didn't give her a name. I saw her in shutter stops and wondered who she was.

Joan and I had soft spells and harsh spells. An edgy momentum carried us. She ducked her head into me and said, "You." She laid on top of me during panic attacks and anchored me to the world. I told her I'd always take care of her. She told me I didn't have to say it so much.

We went to Japan for Joan's 40th birthday. Travel delighted her. Travel bored and angered me. I wanted to contain Joan within hotel rooms and hot-spring baths. I was immune to the beauty around us. I had to close the deal. We flew back to San Francisco, drained and tense. Jet lag sent my world spinning. I poured sweat and took jagged breaths.

Joan suggested a walk. We trekked through Bernal Park and petted dogs as they loped through. I got that sob out. I said, If you let me protect you, you'd be protecting me. Then you wouldn't have to be so harsh and I wouldn't have to be so driven.

It was a ground-zero moment. Joan said nothing.

Fall '05. I live for the Red Goddess that much more.

We had our weekends and weekday phone calls. I had my time alone with Joan's image. Dark rooms contained me and drove me insane.

I saw Joan dancing with strange men. She repeated the sensuous movements that she'd devised for me. I saw her fucking her old lovers. I saw her trawling for black guys. I saw her surfing the Internet for donkey-dicked dudes. The loop endlessly repeated. It would not abate, it would not diminish, it would not cease.

Fight/run, fight/run, fight/run. No one to fight, no haven with Helen, just Joan to run to.

My phone pleas deadened her. My *demands* for softness sickened her. I saw that she had always found me intimidating and pathetic. Her love for me flourished somewhere in between.

We went forward.

We tried.

We knew no quit.

November brought rain. We discussed my potential move to Frisco. We had Thanksgiving dinner with a group of Joan's friends. It was a slow and gracious evening. The people delighted me. I was much older, much taller, not Jewish or left-wing. We celebrated our differences. Joan sat beside me and kept a hand on my knee.

Do it. She'll say "Yes" or "No."

I asked Joan to marry me the next morning. She said, "Yeah." We held each other until our arms numbed.

Helen thought it was nuts. Ditto, my few friends. The divorce finalized on April 20. We set our wedding date for May 13. We had our honeymoon before the ceremony. Christmas in Brooklyn—I meet Joan's family.

It was bittersweet anomaly. I performed and tried to do the right thing. I was ratcheted internally. A new troika raged: wed, impregnate, *contain.*

I moved to Frisco at New Year's. I got a new transition pad near Joan's place. I drifted in and out of most moments. *All* of my moments were raw-nerved. I lived for the Goddess that much more. I could not endure life outside of our embraces. I could not see, think or act beyond the consecration of May 13.

I horrified myself. I wanted to press us into smaller and smaller spaces. I trembled when Joan walked from room to room and withdrew her image.

I lived for May 13.

The country inn. The rings. The red wedding cake. Joan's gown and my ancestral kilt.

I marshaled a horrible will and pushed toward it. I scrounged film deals to cover alimony and the cost of a new home. Troika: the Goddess, Ruth Hilliker, me. The Curse outlived in our child's name.

We marshaled a horrible will and pushed toward it. I saw Joan ratchet internally. I read her mind: misalliance, folie à deux, obsession. He's intimidating, he's pathetic, our worlds collide. He's an amnesiac. He doesn't know where he's been. He's not listening to my answers. His only answer is ME.

My nerves and sleep imploded. The tape show spun. She's dancing, she's fucking black guys, she's seeking monster meat. I could not stop the tapes outside of Joan's presence. I wanted more, more, more and MORE of her.

Joan engaged a therapist to walk us through our shit. The woman liked her and loathed me. Wednesday afternoons under a microscope. Implosive tension—I must fight or run.

I got brusque and outright fucked-up with people. I eyeball-strafed street fools and dared them to GO. The tapes spun. I seized up around Joan and hovered wordless. My inner scream was, *Love me and save me and let me love and save you.* I saw Joan veer toward the word *NO.*

We spent a weekend in Seattle. It was suffocatingly tense. Joan knew a deftly mystical woman. Her specialty: melding antithetical beliefs into seamless wedding vows.

The woman had our number. I saw it plainly. The aging burnout looking for a family. The young woman torn between pity and rage. I saw Joan read the woman's read and veer closer. We flew back to San Francisco. Joan veered *very* close.

She ran.

I don't think I ever could have. Joan always saw me at a sane lover's distance. She was black-clad and had the answer now.

We had a horrible blowup. It explicated all our divisions. It predicted the terrible cost.

It was mutually instigated. It was Joan's pent-up fury and horror at her forfeiture of self. It was my groveling need turned inside out—and a hundredfold shriek of Joan at her most harsh.

She made me leave her apartment. I went back and begged for expressions of love. I threw myself at her door. Joan found a soft voice. She quietly told me to go home and rest.

I did it. She called me three days later and said we were done.

PART V

RAIN

17

Home again.

Cut your losses.

Ghost of a chance.

I looped back to L.A. Twenty-five years, two divorces, one crack-up. The shadows of Helen and Joan. Opportunists require destinations. I didn't know where else to go.

The dream woman lived there. I never got her name. I knew where she worked.

Her first dream appearance was 26 years back. It rained that night. I lost a day's work at the golf course and put the woman in a book. She reappeared at a reading performance. Dreams, visions, potions, elixirs. Witches' brews, vows and bridegrooms in kilts. I believe in this shit. My life testifies to magic and dark-room invocation. *Why the fuck not?*

Her dream *re*appearances occurred during rainstorms. It rained *in* the dreams themselves. I went to church in Frisco just before I left. It rained as I walked out. That cinched the deal.

I was in a post-Joan fugue state. I got weepy over little kids and passed out C-notes to bums. The dream woman nudged me. Go home, motherfucker. You might get lucky.

The dream house sold. Helen and I split a bundle. A

friendship blossomed in our post-divorce wake. Helen praised Joan for dumping my raggedy ass.

Home again. Conjure female spirits in your smog-bound fatherland. I didn't know that women could conjure men. I hadn't met Erika yet.

I dumped transition pad #2 and bought a groovy Porsche. Joan and I had a final good-bye. We held each other and almost collapsed a kitchen chair. We vowed to stay in touch.

I told her that she'd always be my fourth or fifth thought. I underestimated that part of the vow.

My shot nerves and sleep realigned through movement. The assignment of task has always saved me. I rented a two-bedroom apartment and had it decorated. The building adjoined my old peeper turf. The girls' houses stood nearby.

The facades had changed. The faces and floor plans were still vivid. Affluent Asians and film-biz slime had replaced the Hancock Park stiffs.

L.A. was powder blue and bright-light translucent. I sensed a roll with hot dice. L.A. looked like it did the day Jean Hilliker died.

I called the dream woman's place of employment. I ladled some bullshit to an arts czar. The film version of *The Black Dahlia* was nearing release. Would you like me to do a benefit gig?

And, by the way, I met a colleague of yours last year. She was tall. She wore crooked glasses. She came forward in laughter and nearly gasped in retreat.

The arts czar *got* it. Oh, that was Karen. She's married and has a young family. She left our organization and returned to her college post.

A legally wedded professor. The double whammy. A vision, a conundrum, a name.

What the fu—

I'll do the gig. I'm eager to help out. The film opens around Labor Day.

The arts czar was delighted. I asked about Karen's kids. The arts czar said she had two girls.

The pad was a work space/wolf's den. I installed a phone and hung a portrait of Beethoven above the bed. I placed a picture of Helen on my desk and a picture of Joan on my nightstand. The place was deep-hued and dimly lit. I kept the lights off after dusk. Dark rooms bid calls from women. This is sacred text.

Helen and I talked frequently. I called her more than she called me. My solicitude engorged the phone lines. Helen said, Enough—I've got alimony and drama up the ying-yang. Joan and I talked intermittently. Her implied rule: I'll call when I call. I declined dinner invitations and waited in the dark.

Joan's calls played out in three acts. They entailed an allocation of time. Chitchat and the relationship recalled and debriefed. Future career plans.

A reciprocal softness began creeping in. It frightened me. My solitude felt safe. Joan felt like nothing but hurt. I started wanting her all over again. I fought a war of containment. Limit Joan to phone calls. Expand and extol her in the novel. Don't go crazy again. Deliver Joan to History and expunge your own history of misdeeds.

The calls went softer. I played the *Joan* Baez song "Diamonds and Rust" while I waited in the dark. The song described romantic fatality and old lovers as saviors and destroyers.

I sensed another fall impending. I thought about Joan every moment. I played the song obsessively. It was mordant and elegiac. The phone calls went *softer*. I wrote Joan letters. They were *allllll* yearning. The containment war raged. My old jealousies resurfaced. Three consecutive sleepless nights ditzed me. I wrote Joan a horrible note.

I overstated my religiousness and banished her forever. I said I was free-falling and had to save myself. I told her I would pray for her and see her in heaven.

The note worked. It terminated all future contact. The note failed. Joan remained my every second or third thought. The note worked. I stayed sane. The note failed. I still waited for her calls. The note worked. The Red Goddess gave me the throbbing heart of History, revised. The note failed. Joan still lives inside me, full force.

The Black Dahlia bombed. Theaters to cut-rate DVDs at light speed. I didn't care—it sold boocoo books. I did that promised gig. I got to the venue early. Karen and I ran to each other. Her body movements contradicted all her maneuverings in my dreams.

We caught our breath and beamed. We recalled our previous meeting. I told Karen that I schemed the gig to see her again. She laughed and mentioned the kiss that I blew to Joan.

I pretended that you blew me the kiss. What happened to the woman? She was quite lovely.

She dumped my raggedy ass six months ago. How's your marriage?

Karen chortled and went, *Comme ci, comme ça.* Those hot dice scorched my hand. The emcee called me to the lectern. Karen sat in the first row. I gave my speech and H-bombed the room. Karen locked eyes with me. I blew her a kiss. Karen placed her hand on her heart.

· · ·

I didn't think she'd call me. I tagged it as a flirt-and-run. I was life-sentenced to the Joan Zone. Karen was married and had two daughters. I was repentance-wrapped with my ex-wife.

Karen buzzed me. She said the call required Valium and sour mash. She became my third great love.

We met at the Pacific Dining Car. Our embrace was a four-point collision. Helen and I had been married in the next room. The lunch ran three hours. We discussed *Everything*.

Her outer-borough roots. Her Ivy League years. Her historian's focus and the exigent bullshit of the academy. Karen's body language was ambiguous. Likewise, her contradictory talk. She called her marriage and family inviolate. Yeah, but it was a *lust lunch*. We both knew it. Her marriage was malaise-mauled. She didn't say it. I just *knew*.

I left the Dining Car, reeling. Lunch #2 was scheduled for the next week. I full-time brooded on Karen. The Rachmaninoff Preludes, Opus 32, played along. I wrote a song called "Karen Girl." The first line was "Some men were born hungry, some men were born dead—but I was born just to give you head." Karen *looooooooved* it. She was a shit-talker with a Yale Ph.D. We deconstructed history and ragged vile cultural trends. Karen had a tory streak. Karen had insomnia and Ellrovian nerves. Karen was *streeeeeetched thiiiiiiiiiin*. She bombed between her teaching duties and full-time motherhood. She was a task-assigned, duty-driven fucker. My soul screamed, *Ooooooh, baby!!!*

She again said, My marriage and family are inviolate. Fuck that shit. I was already at divorce, our marriage and Daughter #3. Karen refused to rag her husband. I knew why. She was a strong woman hitched to a seed-bearing wimp. She called the shots and let him throw himself at her blank spaces. They were East Coast white ethnics. Family was tsuris. Family was familiar and essential—but Karen craved romantic recognition and schlong. Her compartments had started seeping. She was yours truly, prebreakdown.

Lunch #3 followed. We talked ourselves out fast and laced hands. The gist was, Let's become lovers. Karen stressed, I'm not leaving my husband. I winked and made the jack-off sign.

Adultery.

Adultery with daughters.

Karen on adultery and a future Ellroy child: "The cloven hooves and trident tail would be tough for me."

Adultery with the woman you want for Wife #3.

Adultery: the moral *mishigas* and murky metaphysic. Adultery as priapic prison and dead-end street.

Karen had lost herself in the marriage. It was all kid shit, kid cacophony and middle-aged moms with their boring kid lore. Her work commute ran three hours daily. Her students were all named Mongo Lloyd. Her daughters ran her ragged. Her head was vice-gripped. She needed something all about *her*.

The relationship was restricted to my pad. I understood that Karen's girls came first and drew that line in the sand. We went forward on *her* terms. Her existing commitments demanded it. Karen described her marriage as passionless from Jump Street. She justified our union via that. She was swamped by the results of her reckless search for togetherness and safety. My similar search brought me yet more dark-room solitude as I pushed sixty. Karen wanted recognition. She craved something urgently childless, undomestic and academically unbound. Her nervous energy was my energy—amplified by a *lack* of time alone in the dark.

I understood that adultery was wrong. Karen's sex-dead union gave me my moral road in. I craved marriage with Karen. We were friends at the start. Helen and I had had that. Joan and I had not. "Marriage is sex and courage." Doris Lessing said it. Helen quoted it at our wedding. I threw the quote at Karen. I told her she should not remain in her marriage. It was wrong to pass stasis and romantic dysfunction on to her girls. Her relationship with her husband was moribund. The cocksucker was doomed. My mantra: Divorce your homo hubby and marry me!

We talked, we made love, we became deep friends. We discussed history. I compiled notes for my new novel, *Blood's A Rover.* I studied Karen. I created a Karen-meets-the-Red-Goddess-narrative in my mind. I pre-aged Karen to the age of the fictive Joan Rosen Klein. I retained her adultery and two daughters. I made her a Quaker/leftist/pacifist. My lost daughters with Karen merged with my lost daughter with Joan. My creative world veered toward matriarchy. Motherhood as courage and a road to transcendence. An oddly unveiling late theme for a guy like me.

I learn things late—and only the hard way. My life was a maternal march. Joan and Karen showed me the shortcut to women as History. I had the whole book in my head now.

Dark rooms, phone calls, *Women.*

I called Helen every night. I yearned for Joan non-stop. I brought Joan-yearning to Karen and Karen-lust-overflow to Joan. My multi-woman dreamscape was joyful and un-impeded by hierarchy. Karen and I shared a single nervous system. We were tall, thin and hyper-caffeinated. We could not tamp down, sleep or halt our continuous assessment of meaning. We phone-talked every night. We had hot dates at my love crib twice a week. I mauled Karen with my marry-me mantra. Karen taught me about family.

I'd never had one. That killed Karen. She described her

daughters' lives and her motherly duties as rapture and rav-
aged sprint. Karen persevered within the strictures of a
skunk marriage. She rebuffed my portrayal of said marriage
and spun stories of her girls. The tales rebuffed my ridicule
of their dipshit dad. Karen's girls became my long-sought
children. It was an imaginative construction formed by pillow talk. It was free of the swerving fears of *real* parenthood
and all the daily drudge work. I mythologized two kids I
had never met. Karen and I riffed off their established per-
sonalities and gave them gleeful fantasy lives. They were the
henchbabies of southside dope dealers and sold black-
market nukes. They robbed pharmacies and peddled pills to
their nursery school chums. Karen and I laughed our fucking asses off.

We had fun. I left Karen raucous phone messages. Hey,
baby—LAPD's surveilling your hubby. I've got my minions
out to frame him. He's cruising gay bars. He's been to the
Manhole, the Cockpit, the Rump Room and Boys "R" Us.
Karen loved this shit. Karen howled and roared. I kept up
my marry-me mantra. Karen said, No, no, NO.

It got to me. I wanted more. I loved Karen. We were
lovers *and* friends. I hadn't met her daughters. They were
old enough to rat me to the hubby. All my crazy Joan shit
got re-constellated and re-themed.

Karen's out dancing, Karen's nude hot-tubbing, Karen's
fucking black guys and seeking monster meat. My nerves
sheared, my sleep tanked, my brain spun that tape.

It was frantic phone calls, panic attacks and sobs in the
dark. Karen consoled me and said, No, no, NO. I begged,
pleaded, scrutinized, importuned, cajoled, dissected, ana-
lyzed and begged and pleaded anew. I hit a wall at Christmas '06.

Karen went back east with her family. I drove to Carmel
and crashed in Helen's garage. Margaret barked and

growled at me. I pondered a Frisco run to peep Joan. I moped around. Helen kicked me and said, "Quit mooning for your married girlfriend, you fuck."

I went through a week of Yuletide moans in the night. I sat down to start the outline for the novel. The themes and characters jumped out, boldfaced.

Lost mothers, lost children, Karen Sifakis and Joan Klein. Helen's edict to write more from the heart. History as redeeming fire. The great male urge to atone for misdeeds. *Women as the ever-present grail and payoff. Women as the proactive voice of revolution.*

I called Karen back east. I marry-me mantraed her a last time. She said, No, no, NO. I said, Let's segue into a friendship. She said, Please don't bail on me. I said, Not a chance.

Karen didn't bail. I didn't bail. We spoke every night. We had coffee, lunch or dinner twice a week. We hogged a back booth at the Pacific Dining Car and talked heavy-duty shit.

She said, "Do you really believe that you conjured me?"

I said, "Yes, I do."

"You saw me in a dream and put me in a book."

"That's correct. It rained that night. I saw you quite vividly."

"And you weren't at all surprised when you met me twenty-odd years later?"

"No. Prophecy is a by-product of my extreme single-mindedness and the cultivation of solitude."

"So you uprooted to L.A., to pursue a married woman you'd met for two seconds?"

"That's correct."

"And you did not really expect that we'd become lovers."

"No. I had to get out of San Francisco. L.A. seemed like a good idea."

"Because you have friends and film colleagues here?"

"No."

"Because you're from here, and it's where you're the most well known?"

"No. Those are not sufficient reasons."

"You're saying . . ."

"I'm saying I had a dream and met the dream woman in the flesh. I'm saying, 'Why the fuck not?' "

"Do women possess conjuring powers, or is this strictly a male preserve?"

"I don't know."

"What would you do if a woman conjured your skinny ass out of the *spiritus mundi* and did a number on you like you did on me?"

"I'd brood and pray. I'd assess her character. I'd ponder her acuity and her intuitive powers very carefully."

"And if she passed all those tests?"

"I'd capitulate."

The friendship pact was formed at New Year's '07. I worked on my book and got tighter with Karen and Helen. They met once. They liked each other. Helen told Karen to get smart. Divorce your fruit husband—but don't marry Ellroy.

I vowed to give up chasing for Lent. I wanted to reseal my thoughts within a love/sex ban. I wanted to see how my brain and soul waves might shift as I stumbled toward 60.

Karen and I stuck in. We talked funny shit and profound shit. Most of our moments were freighted with loss and longing. Every other moment impishly implied irony.

I'd ask Karen, "Do you love me?"

She'd say, "I'll think about it."

I'd get frustrated. I'd say, "Divorce your fruit husband and marry me."

She'd say, "You don't understand family. All you've got is your audience and your prey."

I laughed and winced. Karen was right. Those factions comprised my whole world. Karen recalled our talk on dream states and female summoning. She said, "For a right-wing religious nut, you've always seemed to lack faith."

PART VI

HER

I said, "You knew before I did. That's what gets me."

She said, "You're saying that you always know before the woman does?"

"Yes."

"It's called 'projection.' It's why standard gender roles have remained in place for eons."

"I hate to consider myself predictable."

"You're not. Your single-mindedness is so furious that it recasts projection and puts you in an entirely different league."

"And you knew that?"

"Immediately."

"That first day we met?"

"Instantly."

"You were married. You had two daughters."

"When has that ever stopped you?"

"You might have considered it a pathologically ingrained pattern. I'm stating a phrase my friend Karen might use when I describe you to her."

"Your pathology is possessed of grandeur. I appreciated that."

"Your marriage is Karen's marriage. You married a safe guy and went for the okeydoke. It's called 'projection,' and it's why standard gender roles have remained in place for eons."

"Thank you for patronizing me without sufficient knowledge of my husband and daughters."

"I've always wanted a daughter."

"Yes. I know that."

"When did you figure it out?"

"The second time I met you."

"A year later?"

"Yes."

"We discussed daughters that time."

"It wasn't the topic of discussion. It was your eyes."

"Divorce your fruit husband and marry me."

"Don't recycle your old married-lover shtick."

"We aren't lovers."

"No. And we probably never will be."

"We're blowing our vibe. Let's get back to 'You knew before I did.'"

"I thought, 'That is the only man I have ever met who is as love-hungry as me.'"

18

Faith and self-will clash and fuel me. Abstinence releases a magical flow. Helen and Karen remained my best friends. They harped on the faith-versus-will issue and applauded my Lent '07 plunge.

Asceticism and lust clash and fuel me. That conflict and my extremely narrow focus create great discomfort and bursts of inner peace. Winter '07 was my past recaptured and my writing future remapped. I lived in a superbly appointed apartment. It was 14 blocks from the dog-shit dive where I'd lived 45 years back. It was spotlessly clean and tidy. The only books on shelves were my own books. There were no family portraits. I possessed one photo each of Helen, Karen and Joan. Beethoven portraits loomed on walls and counters. I had a high-line boom box and no TV, computer or cell phone. The pad was bereft of extraneous objects. I mimicked Christ's sojourn in the desert on a lush leather couch. The geography of L.A. *then* cradled me *now*. I time-machined back to a fictional L.A. before my postwar novels and my birth. I began to envision Jean Hilliker within a new *fictional* context. I abstained from seeking women who resembled her, refracted her, absorbed her or diverted and allayed the shock value and spiritual content of her life. Her image bushwhacked me constantly. Vivid period settings evolved each time she appeared. I conceived a quartet of novels, larger in scope than anything I had thus far achieved. I danced with my mother's ghost and walked from room to room in the dark. I felt time and space as her sole continuum. Lent came and went. I met a woman four days after Easter. Helen and Karen were skeptical.

Helen said, "Mr. Restraint."

Karen said, "What took you so long?"

She was a lovely woman. It felt un-kosher, nonetheless. My mojo was off. I was horny, predatory and preachily pristine. I was off in matriarchal mania. I was writing a big novel and planning four bigger ones. Joan and Karen ruled the current book and most of the men in it. Jean Hilliker loomed as fictive deity.

I liked the new woman. She found me dubious. She was gracious, she was charming, she was naturally restrained.

My herky-jerky momentum unnerved her. I was trying to be proper and reinvest in sex.

Be courtly. Meander and milk the moment for meaning. Pile on the pianissimo and postpone the pizzazz.

I bumbled and poked around in the woman's murky places. I craved drama and tried to shed some blood, à la the Red Goddess Joan. The woman was a writer. We had same-day gigs at the *L.A. Times* book fair. I arrived before her and hobknobbed with folks in the greenroom. I motor-mouthed per the woman and our emerging grand passion. I was selling myself a bill of goods. *I knew it then.* I knew the woman was not The Woman and could not pick up the tab for me. I was resurrection-razzed and chaliced by chastity. I was love-starved and full of shit.

The greenroom buzzed. I chatted with some people. We stood with plates and book-gabbed. A man and a woman stood to my right. A woman stood to my left. She was tall and had reddish blond hair. She was in her early to mid-forties. Her features were stern, with odd and quite lovely swerves. She ate chili. I observed her. I watched her resist the urge to bite her nails. It delighted me.

Her eyes were no-shit, non-hazel green. Her body was sleek, with surprisingly voluptuous swerves. I knew I'd ponder her in the dark, habitually.

Her first name was Erika. Her surname denoted a pedigree. She had a flash-in-the-pan novelist mother of '70s vintage and a famous film-critic dad. She was a journalist. She had published a *mom*oir during a recent motherhood-as-crucifixion-and-ecstasy book craze. She was married and had two daughters. I thought, *That is one big, good-looking motherfucker*—and blathered on about my latest folie à deux.

Married. Two daughters. Shit—I've been *there*. A sound track kicked on and broiled my brain waves. It wasn't Beethoven—it was all bubblegum.

The Grass Roots with "Sooner Or Later." Lou Christie with "I'm Gonna Make You Mine."

Erika recalled the moment two years and three months later. She said, "I thought, 'He should not be with that woman. He should be with me.' "

My reinvestment in sex and decorous romance went bankrupt. It was a pyramid scheme built on high hopes and hopped-up hormones. I tried. The woman tried. We attempted to merge our emotional assets and failed. We were wrong for each other. It was a short-sell scenario. It was all suspension of disbelief.

Erika learned that the deal tanked. She recalled the gossip two years and four months later. She said, "I knew it wouldn't last. I knew you should be with me."

Karen and I *again* reinvested. That didn't fly. We had months-long on-and-off stints. I pressured Karen to leave her fruit husband. She persistently refused. We hit the off switch and settled into a long-standing friendship. I wrote my novel and burned for the historically revised Karen and Joan. *They* gave me daughters. Karen's real-life daughter tales weaved through the text.

I was full of dumb-shit kid love and no one to give it to. I was turning sixty, with a teenage sex drive. I went out to dinner alone every night. I chose the restaurants on one basis only. Will a Jewish woman with dark, gray-streaked hair show up here? Will she be older and softer than Joan? Will she not be afraid of me?

The wish-named Joan, the real Joan, the Red Goddess in my book. A dozen L.A. restaurants as the No-Joan Zone.

I had dumb-ass liaisons. My attempts to make the wrong woman right triggered physical backlash. I trembled during bedroom excursions. I had panic attacks worse than the vintage '01 jobs. I glimpsed women in restaurants and sent them gooey notes. They *all* blew me off. I flew to France and Great Britain—determined to wed, impregnate, *contain.* I moved to New York for a brief spell and attempted to levy the troika there. It all hurt. I fucked over good women. I was always tensed up to fight or run.

It's not a fight. Love shouldn't hurt. Erika told me that last night.

My novel describes History as a state of yearning. The writing of it tossed my yearning patterns every which way. I'd try to conjure faces and come up blank. I'd see Erika, propped up on her elbows beside me. She appeared persistently. She always wore blue jeans and nothing else. Her breasts brushed the bedcovers. Her undress and avid gestures whooshed as willpower, brainpower and Big Sex. Erika was my inconsistent companion in the dark. I had met her only once. I kept wondering what she meant.

I inquired about her. Mutual acquaintances provided

snapshots. Literary folks distrusted her. She was an opportunist. She had a flamboyant and loudmouthed side. I got a vibe.

If you can't love me, notice me. That staple from troubled-childhood textbooks. Possibly true of Erika, definitive of me.

The husband, the two daughters. Karen turf. I wasn't up for another married-woman shitkicking—

Yet.

I ignored all stated opinions of Erika. I knew that she was better than the extant scuttlebutt. I knew that she was kind and true. She kept showing up inside me. Her appearances were sporadic *and* purposeful. She existed outside of me and materialized at her—not my—will. I began to sense this mental flight plan as uniquely indigenous to Erika herself.

There she is. She's on the bedcovers. I've got a sense that she knows things I don't.

I attended the *Times* book fair in 2008. I looked for Erika and found her. She was delighted that I recalled her. I inquired about her daughters. Her answers ripped me up. She described two arty girls and a kids' production of *Peter Pan.*

"You were my *human*, Ellroy. I knew it then," Erika said that last week.

We knew people in overlapping circles. I laid out I-dig-her parries and got she-digs-you ones back. I grooved the process. It was très junior high school. Most people winced to indicate film noir fatality. People said, "She's *married.*" More film noir shtick unfurled. I got what people got about the notion of us. Our shared flamboyance and opportunism. The inconvenient husband, the gas chamber in six months.

I probed per the marriage. I logged evasions and winces. I got the gestalt:

Tanker. Call Erika's marriage the Exxon Valdez. It's headed for environmental grief.

It was June '08. A friend invited me to a party. I said, "Will Erika be there?" My friend said, "Yes."

I said, "*I'll* be there."

I went to the party. Erika did not appear. She continued to crash my brood sessions. She appeared persistently. Fuck—she's shirtless and up on her elbows. It's not obsession or conjuring—it's just fucking *Her*.

Her cadences eluded me. I didn't know what she meant.

I spent Christmas '08 in New York. I stood at Rockefeller Center and watched fortyish moms and their daughters ice-skate. Helen met Erika at a party in L.A. They had a lovely chat. I asked Helen to describe the conversation. She smiled and mock-sealed her lips.

There she is. She's on the bedcovers. She's telling you things.

We had amazing conversations. Her green eyes grabbed me. Her gestures were more forceful than those of any other woman who had ever joined me in the dark.

I finished my novel. It embodied Joan, Karen and daughters unfound. The weight of my years and my native kid verve coalesced. I felt swervy and out of control. That Rilke quote kept popping up: "You must change your life."

I knew that I had to change. I sensed that I *could* change. I had to hurl my God sense and word self at The Curse.

It came to me in the dark. The revelation occurred between phone calls with Helen and Karen. Marcia Sidwell had drifted by. A flow of faces followed her. Jean Hilliker morphed out of them. Erika was propped up beside me. I had just thought about Joan.

19

So women will love me.

Jean Hilliker would be 95 now. The Curse is 52 years old. I have spent five decades in search of one woman to destroy a myth. That myth was self-created and speciously defined. I imposed a narrative line to ensure my own survival. It levied blame to suppress grief and vouchsafe my crazy passion. The Curse was half a blessing. I've survived just fine.

So women will love me.

It's a fine raison d'être. It's kept me hungry and working hard. I am predisposed to rash and thoughtless acts in love's name. This memoir will help me to interdict the practice. I require strict boundaries. They serve to curtail my ardent resolve and grandiosity. The inward gaze has always pushed me outward toward Them. It's often delusional and occasionally a ticket to a state of grace.

I have now set a bar that will mandate circumspection. The dominant story line of my life will dissolve on the last page I write here. The preceding pages have been me in address of Her and Them. It's time to put down my pen and live from Their sole perspective. I must sit alone in the dark. They must come to me sans conjuring or images recalled and transposed. They may say nothing. They may tell me that I have always possessed an unfathomable fate. God engages me through women. My task has always been to bring women to God. This pursuit has pushed me toward self-serving error. They have slowly and persistently revealed the cost of my actions. I must sit alone with Them now and will myself receptive. They have formed a sisterhood within me. I am steeled for Their rebukes and open-armed for any messengers They may send me. I'm getting past the shallow breaths at the core of my quest.

I exist in a matriarchy. I'm the lost boy rescued and cut loose by strong women. I outgrew him as I told his story. I always write my way through to the truth. I believe it because Helen Knode said so.

I talk to Helen and Karen most nights. Helen just moved to Austin, Texas. Margaret barks at me, long-distance. Karen's still married to her fruit husband. I've quit pestering her about it. We've kept it clean for some time now. Karen still comes forward in laughter and nearly gasps in retreat.

Joan had a child last year. I've heard conflicting reports of the kid's gender. I suspect it's a boy and hope it's a girl. I'm clueless per the patrimony. I want it to stay that way. History is the smallest of the many gifts Joan gave me. She earned her prominence and paid for it dearly. She's a far-off fixed star now.

Joan never calls me. A woman named Julia does. She's 29, she's brilliant, she's a lesbian. We look alike. She's my spiritual daughter. We have dinner and talk profound shit about women. Restaurant people assume my patrimony. It's heartbreaking. I met her at the *L.A. Times* book fair, 2009. I went there to give a speech. I had dressed for Erika.

I was *armed* for Erika. I wanted to go someplace quiet and contained with her. I wanted to look at her and let our hands brush across a table. She's married, I'm not. Who'll pull their hand back first?

It's been two years now.

I'm exhausted with my crazy shit.

We comprise a significant courtship. Your appearances are inimitable. Are you thinking about me?

20

I gave the speech. It was a fucking barn burner. I wore a blue-and-white-striped seersucker suit, a white shirt and a tartan bow tie. I looked handsome as shit. I never saw Erika. I prowled the greenroom and the area surrounding. My dream lover was nowhere.

Erika dressed for me at that Christmas party. She described the shoes that put her up at six one and the shoulderless black dress. We laughed about it last night. Erika said, "I met your ex-wife instead."

She knew it first.

She summoned me.

She sought me alone in the dark. She spent over two years in the pursuit. She practiced the conjuror's art with greater persistence and acuity than I did. She knew more about me than I sensed about her. Her knowledge superseded a glut of rumors and published text. Her insight outweighed my self-awareness. She came better armed. Her preeminent commitment, first formed in solitude, has enjoined us and sealed our romantic fate.

She willed me. I lacked the fortitude and certain knowledge that fueled her will. She knew she could outwill me. A confrontation was required. I had failed to accomplish that task. Erika knew how to do it.

My publisher hooked me up to Facebook. They knew

my aversion to computers and coerced me into it. My job was to ballyhoo my new novel all over cyberspace. A colleague told me that people posted "friend" requests that I must reject or confirm. I performed this boring duty for three weeks. It was deadening shit work. Then Erika's name and image hit my colleague's computer screen.

I whooped. I hit the confirm button. I composed an ardent poem in rhyming Old English. I pushed the send button. I waited a full day. Erika sent me a note back.

She was surprised, she was thankful, she was delighted. She included a perfunctory aside on her marriage. She left room for me to wedge my snout back in her Internet door.

I sent her a more ardent poem. Her reply gently rebuked me.

Yeah, I dig you. But, I'm happily married. I've got two daughters. We have too many friends in common. You're too notoriously obsessive. It's not worth the risk.

I Internet-apologized. Erika e-mail-accepted my mock retreat. She bemoaned her current psychic state. I slashed at the critque. I *knew* her. I *knew* her marriage was tanksville. I *knew* the extent of the crazy shit in *her* head. I *sensed* what *she knew* first: This person is a cut-from-the-bone version of my flawed and transcendence-seeking self.

Erika wrote me again. She dissected my most recent TV performance. I was nervy and pervy. My ego staggered her. I exemplified a particularly male strain of arrested development. *But*—she still felt *compelled*.

The e-mail was a wounder. I wrote back and offered to splitsville for good. I had called her "my seditious sister." Erika wrote, "So it is with great regret that I must banish you, my brazen brother."

I moped a little. I quickly revitalized. Give up? *Fuck that shit!*

I waited two weeks. I thought about Erika, non-stop.

She had implied her own two-year conjuring. I conjured her conjuring and got an idea. It came to me. Not surprisingly—alone in the dark.

Erika was unparalleled in my passion pantheon. Our chaste courtship was two-plus years in. She might have her own belief in invisibility. She possessed wild perceptive powers. Her wavery skepticism demonstrated that. All our detractors would dispute it—but—*now I know.*

This woman is the female embodiment of your inner soul. You must address her in the voice of the most urgent artist in history.

Thus: this aging horndog writes as Beethoven. Thus: Erika becomes his "Immortal Beloved." Thus: cyberspace becomes Vienna, 1810.

I went at it with bombast and glee. The letter reeked of the staggering ego that Erika glimpsed on TV. My mere identification with the Master announced my megalomania. The built-in gasp-and-yuck factor was enormous. Softness underscored it. I was a journeyman yearner. I assumed the voice of the greatest yearner of all fucking time. Erika was a yearner. She lived in the soft passages of the "Les Adieux" Sonata, whether she had ever heard it or not. She understood unexpressed desire and the sweetness-sadness parlay that is art. The years were 1810 and 2009. I added a jolt of 1962. I was a junior high school window-peeper, adrift. Erika was the mother of all the Hancock Park girls combined. She was all the society ladies I peeped at that Twist party. She was vexed, unbodied and riddled with ennui. Her height and carriage connoted Anne Sexton. She was 45, I was 61. She was every older woman I had youthfully glimpsed and craved. I was significantly older than her now. I was far further into the back nine of life. The letter was a cri de coeur and a treatise on ephemera, cut through with a blast of the "Peppermint Twist."

I wrote it. I sent it. Erika wrote back, immediately. She expressed reluctant pleasure. She praised the dramatic construction and ridiculed my "Immortal Beloved" casting. She guardedly invited me to contact her again.

A daily correspondence commenced. I handwrote letters and faxed them to Erika's computer. Erika sent typed faxes back. I pursued. Erika advanced and retreated at an unpredictable pace. She cited my reputation as a grandstander, womanizer and right-wing buffoon. I tried to differentiate my public and private personae. I unloaded the truth of my life. I requested reciprocity. Erika complied. She described her life as seeping compartments and looming icebergs. She was a one-book wonder with a second memoir in perilous rough draft. Her daughters were 11 and 14. Motherhood was exaltation and drudge work. Read *my* book. Motherhood is *my* shtick—just like *dead* mothers are yours.

I love my daughters. They're always there. They're just like She is for you.

Yes, but they're alive. They're more real than Her. They're children. They devour your everydays. They're not this ghost I dance with at whim.

I spend my time with car pools and Girl Scout troops. I write intermittently. You're correct about my marriage. It's been in unbreachable stasis for years. I'm fucked behind inertia. Your brutal will moves and horrifies me. I wonder who you are in your heart.

I'm fearful. I'm domineering and unsocialized. I lure people in and push them away. I write obsessively and with great concision. I'm religious and possess social views you would surely find appalling. All I want is intense communion with women and time alone in the dark.

Letters went out. Letters came in. I sent Erika my phone number. She declined to send me hers. I pursued. She resisted. I retreated in a decorous fashion. Erika rewarded me with lovely compliments. I felt hot-wired to God. Erika bid me to virtue as we committed a text-tailed adultery. We decoded each other sans benefit of voice, sight and touch. Our letters deludedly banished the prospect of sex—as we rushed toward it in platonic love's name.

She called me. It was 11:00 p.m. on a Monday. Our courtship was one month in.

She said, "Hi, it's Erika." She was in her car, parked near her house. It reeked of cheating. Her voice startled me. It countermanded the tone of her letters. Some bottom dropped out of me. It was queasiness meets weightlessness. Small talk dribbled out and took us nowhere. Spoken discourse contradicted the heft of our words on paper. I thought we'd get to big themes fast. I came on judgmental. Erika felt foolish and overmatched. We both went borderline hostile.

The chat lasted ninety minutes. I hung up and crashed on my bed. The room spun. My pulse went triple its normal rate.

We went back to writing. I assumed Erika's perspective. She was cheating. Her herky-jerky chatter and long pauses made that plain. Her new faxes confirmed my assessment. *Fucker, I called you. I've got more to lose than you have. This is not easy.*

She said that she'd call again. I knew she would. Leave the lights off and wait by the phone. It *will* ring. You'll *make* it ring. You've got it equally bad for each other.

Our rapport accelerated via the written word. The main theme was change. The question was, How do we change *each other*? My outer life was all success and well-earned recognition. My inner life was lonely turmoil and obsessive ambition and lust. Erika had a moribund marriage. She'd lived a wild early life and became horrified at her penchant for chaos. She married a sweet-natured man and set out to redeem him and create a safe-love zone. The man failed to fulfill Erika's fatuous expectations. She felt guilty and unreasonably responsible for his psychic state. The union was decidedly over. The two bright and lovely daughters were daily compensations and a brutal workload all to themselves. Erika lived in despair. She built her own cage and stared through the gaps in the bars. Her daughters provided work furlough. There was a dear joy in it—and more and more work. She carried the bulk of the weight in the marriage. She took full responsibility for the state of the union and assigned her husband no blame. Her native joie de vivre was going, going, gone. She possessed a heroic soul. She was Beethovian in her schizy grasp at life in all its horror and beauty. She humbled me. I was male and unencumbered. I cut and ran from dicey entanglements and lived full-time in my head. I was a man. Gender bias had favored me.

You know your job. Work hard to quash other men and render them sterile. Dream enormous dreams and seek women. Many men do this. *You* do it with unique verve and efficacy. Now you're 61 and waiting in the dark for another married mother to call you. Isn't that pathetic? Aren't you ashamed?

No, not really.

I'm in a sacred fight now. There's her as Her and something else, and if we continue to tell the truth, we'll both win.

Erika called me again. The conversation went more smoothly. We had accepted the weightiness and open-endedness of the attachment and considered the emergent US to be a spiritual entity. Erika railed at my media antics. I railed at her willingness to live in dysfunction. It reigned as subtext: We're out to saw off the chains that constrain our souls—but we can't fuck.

Our correspondence was six weeks in. My fax machine

and Erika's computer worked overtime. Erika flew back east to visit her sister. We scorched the phone lines from L.A. to Chagrin Falls, Ohio.

We discussed *everything*. Our talks ran for hours. We detailed our promiscuous pasts and argued politics. We ping-ponged between We're already lovers, No, we're not, and Who are we kidding? Erika discussed her daughters. I admitted my incapacity for fatherhood and conceded that children as redemption for murdered mothers was a truly nutty ideal. We talked lots of sizzling sex shit. We kept trying to define what we were and finally gave up. We told each other "I love you" at the end of every phone call—*and meant it.*

I didn't care who we were.

I required no consummation.

I knew that whoever we were and whatever we had would never stop.

I told Karen about Erika. She said, "I used to think you were smart." I told Helen about Erika. Helen noted her marked resemblance to Jean Hilliker. I noted her marked resemblance to yours truly.

Erika said, "What do we do now?"

I said, "We tell the truth."

The courtship was seven weeks in. We hadn't seen each other in one year and three months.

The phone rang. It was midweek at 3:00 p.m. Erika said, "Hello." I blurted, "Coffee? Le Pain Quotidien at 1st and Larchmont?" She said, "Half an hour?"

A faux-rustic coffee cave. Overpriced java and overdressed pastry. Overlit in faux-Provence colors. Not the backdrop for film noir fatality.

But it was.

Because it was *over* then.

Film noir is an over-referenced genre. Adultery rarely ends in the greenroom at Big Q. Divorce court is a more likely destination. Pellets don't drop into acid vats. People weep and rage and try to determine where things went wrong. People try to figure out how to get things right.

I arrived first. The table was at the back, with a front-entrance view. She walked in five minutes later. She wore a look that I've come to love and that Erika first formally noted. "If I'm not smiling, I look frightened, worried or stern."

She wasn't smiling. It didn't matter. She was the loveliest woman I had ever seen.

We embraced. We held each other 47 beats too long. We sat down. We didn't hold hands. We leaned across the table and laced up our arms.

Two hours dissolved into microseconds. Self-absorbed *memoirists*? All we talked about was *US*.

It was natural.

It was easy.

The flow was evenly deployed. Two self-obsessed memoirists—and no one talked too much.

Who are we? What are we? Should we do it? Fuck—my husband and kids. It doesn't feel wrong—it feels sweet. My husband, my kids, the censure I'll face, your shitty reputation.

Your shitty rep and your murdered-mom miasma. Everyone will think I'm insane—but I have no doubt you're the one.

I said, "I'll help you with your manuscript."

She said, "Whatever happens, I don't ever want to lose you."

Those green eyes. Those beautiful big hands. Her buoyancy in the face of years of disappointment. My retreat into her glow.

She called me "Ellroy." It was a distancing device. I

addressed her as "Darling" more than "Erika." I said, "I want to buy you a black cashmere dress." She said, "Don't do shit you've done with other women. It would fucking kill me."

I walked Erika back to her car. Our good-bye embrace lasted 48 beats too long. She held me very tightly. My hands played over the long sweep of her back.

Other women blurred and faded altogether. *Blood's A Rover* neared publication. The dedication to Joan receded as a milestone event. I pondered Erika. I resisted the urge to recast her in my own image. A shared resemblance asserted itself even as I tried to refrain. The backlash was a soft truth set off by whispers, jingles and gongs. She's big and clumsy. So are you. She's sweet-natured and often appears harsh. She observes moments as she lives them. You're that way. She's afraid to love and more afraid not to. She's indefatigable and dutiful. She loves to put unequivocal and somewhat shocking words on paper. Now she's writing them to you.

She's short-sold herself to the world. You've over-sold yourself. You diverge there. You have told each other the truth for over two months now. You have fought for comportment. She knows your whole Karen story. She knows that you can't tread that route again.

I studied Erika formally. The absence of sex fueled my study. She was *grateful*. She swooned at any dollop of recognition. Her harshness was a defensive posture and a moment-to-moment stance to propel her through the prosaic tasks of the world. She was impeccably gracious. She apologized for herself, without necessity. She jive-talked better than Karen and Helen Knode. I read her memoir. She was singularly perceptive and in surefire control of the autobiographical essay. This evinced her life in the constant assessment of meaning. Her retreat mode was dirty-girl talk for shock value. She was Ellrovian that way. If you can't love me, notice me. Give us a microphone and an audience and self-inflicted harm *will* ensue. Erika was on a harrowing human journey. She was deadeningly encumbered by people she loved dearly. She had all my crazy exhibitionistic bullshit pegged. She understood it because we shared that psychic componentry. *This was courtship.* We had two months of words, concepts and tones decoded. Our souls were locked as one. Our bodies had yet to follow.

We're not even formal lovers. It was a long shot two months ago. I'm getting the vibe—*she just might have the stones to jump.*

We began meeting at my pad. We sat at the kitchen table and reviewed her manuscript. It was a woman's-whole-life book couched as a coming-of-age memoir. I'd heard some of the stories anecdotally. Erika's tale of exile and neglect was my story with the volume dimmed, upscale backdrops and no curse and resultant murder. We converged again. Erika told me the tale of her marriage. She included the through-line that Karen always omitted. We converged *and* diverged there. I never demonized or ridiculed Erika's husband. I knew she wouldn't tolerate it. He was a good man in the thrall of a powerful and powerfully tormented woman. I knew that our collective mandate was to change each other. We were attempting to merge into a symbiotic and non-codependent whole—whatever the parameters of our union.

We were united for that express purpose. It eclipsed sexual conjunction and anointed us with a solar system–high calling. We had to become the best parts of each other. I had to learn tolerance and greater humility. Erika required a transfusion of my determination and drive. I believed it because I knew it to be real beyond all manifestations of madness in my woman-mad life to date. Erika considered us cosmic. She repeatedly told me that our bond did not feel wrong. Her friendly love for her husband did not enrage me. They were comrades and parents united by shared history and ripped apart by a stultifying isolation. Their commitment to their daughters was a full-time job all its own. Seasoned adulterer Ellroy knew this. Neophyte Erika knew that she should not pass her marital legacy to her girls. That common meeting ground in no way astonished me. The newly confrontational woman had *changed*. She could not run and hide like she used to. Nor could I. She had changed *me*. I now inhabited a romantic world with no prescribed borders. This astonished me: I loved Erika past all expectations.

Her manuscript required revisions. We worked at the table. It adjoined the living room and a long leather couch. Erika suggested an afternoon nap there. I gleefully acceded to the suggestion. There we were. The fit was tight. Erika threw a leg over me. My heart trip-hammered. Erika placed her head on my shoulder. We avoided eye contact that might lead to a kiss.

Reinvestment.

Fierce hearts beating. Let's Twist again. Junior high limits adhered to—2009 as 1962.

The summer wore on. We were nine weeks into our courtship. It was hot. The couch got too sticky. We curled up on the bed. Contact accelerated.

We *still* imposed limits. We stretched out crossways and let our long legs dangle over the edge. The crossways pose became untenable. Two weeks of it was wracking our shins. We moved up and placed our heads on the pillows. Erika's eyes were very close.

She played me a song her 14-year-old daughter had written. It was a sweet and melodic love tune. Her daughter strummed a ukulele. Her voice broke during the high notes. I started crying. Erika leaned in. I kissed her then.

She jumped.

She was on her way back from a family vacation. Their car overheated and stranded them in Fresno in a heat wave. They dined en famille at a Rally's Burger dump. The girls scrounged trinkets at a 99¢ Only Store. Erika and her husband sat on a grassy strip nearby. A dog turd reposed a few feet away. Erika picked it up with a Rally's Burger wrapper and trash-canned it.

She told him. He took it hard. That was mid-August. It's now the following June.

We've been together since then.

21

It's who she is.

It's who she was and who she's becoming.

It's the fact that *she* summoned *me*.

Erika moved to a new pad near her old house. The girls took it hard and rebounded. The husband's rebounding. He's got a new girlfriend. Erika's fighting off waves of residual guilt and regret. I buck her up with sociopathic good cheer.

Marriage hits the rocks. Choppy seas pushed the boat there. Both of you were complicit. You both fought for the wheel.

Divorce isn't so bad. I've done it twice myself. Three's my lucky number. Wear my tartan sash at our wedding—or at least *think* about it.

My few friends express disbelief. Helen cites the "Tall Redhead Syndrome." Karen says, "You finally destroyed a marriage. Mazel-fucking-tov." The bulk of Erika's many friends have censured her. You left that sweet man for *him*?

I keep asking Erika to say it. Please, darling. Say it again.

Yes, baby. You're absolutely right. This is the sweetest shit that's ever been.

We've told each other the truth for a year now. Our most potent shared trait is gratitude. We read each other's eyes and offer reassurance telepathically. We are dominant people possessed of frail contours and bottomless need. We are unassuageably hungry for each other and concommitantly as soft. Call us bubblegummers scaling the Mountain of Love. Call us passion's pilgrims unbound.

I'm fond of Erika's daughters. The creation of two separate households have stretched them thin. They are wary of me and sometimes look askance at their mother and the odd man she hooked up with. I'm deferential to both girls. I crack a few jokes, work to amuse them and leave them alone. I push no I'm-your-dad agenda. They seem to respect me for that. I make their mother happy. I seem to score points there. I would never tell them that their presence marks the closest that I've ever come to Family.

I'm not their father, or anyone's father. Fatherhood would have been a giant tank job for me. The elder daughter smiled at me yesterday. She didn't have to. *I think I get it.* Moments like that accrete and melt you. Biological connection is unnecessary. I bought the younger daughter a stuffed alligator. I speak to him in jive talk. The reward is a few offhand yucks. More moments will accumulate. I'm triply blessed. The woman I love has mothered two superb children. They are eminently worthy of their own determined contemplation. They're children. They set a bar of propriety. The memoirists and self-obsessed lovers must rise to it.

Our collective friends think we'll flame out. They point to Erika's girls as collateral victims. Many of Erika's friends have scarlet-lettered her. An expressed "Fuck You All" would feel good in the moment and backfire in the end.

Erika gets fearful. We diverge in many ways. She's social and omnivorously connected to the world. I'm very reclusive. All I want is Erika enclosed within small spaces and time alone with her in the dark. *I* get fearful. I'm jealous and possessive. I'm always scanning for predators out to take my woman away. Erika talks to me softly and loves me out into the world. I'm often tensed up to fight. I'm rarely tensed up to run. I ran toward Erika for 50 years. I will not run away from her now.

We are divinely deigned. Our bodiment was purchased by a mutual recklessness and refusal to forfeit belief in love. Together, we are sex and courage. Alone, we were skewed strains of self-will.

I'm no good without her. She's no good without me. I had always considered that a weakling's epigram. I was surely mistaken.

Tell me again, please.

Yes, baby. This is the sweetest shit that's ever been.

Erika stepped out of the shower yesterday morning. Her wet hair was auburn-hued. She dried it off and cinched it back. She looked startlingly like Jean Hilliker.

We scrabble at building a day-to-day life. It's easier for Erika than it's been for me. I'm becoming socialized. Erika has resisted my attempts to four-wall us into containment. We engage a range of activities and always return to a dark, enclosed space. She knows it's all I want. She wants something besides that. I'm getting better. Our union has a greater shot at success if we maneuver in the world— clothed, on occasion. We always end up alone and enfolded. My nerves always decelerate as we get to my place or her place and the locks click.

There's things you must learn. You've taken me very far. Let me give you a primer on life outside of your head.

Yes, darling—if you say it, then I know it's true.

I've met Erika's soon-to-be ex-husband on two occasions. He personifies graciousness and concedes that we all did the right thing. He embodies a unique strain of the gratitude that I have always sought. He has lessons to teach me.

I always get what I want. I more often than not suffocate or discard what I want the most. It cuts me loose to yearn and profitably repeat the pattern. Erika is teaching me to interdict this practice. I've never been loved or taught this gently or with this much precision or decorum. My moments of railing and retreat. Her confrontations that bring me back to the truth. Our belief that such moments will allow our moments to extend and our union to last.

Erika often notes our cosmic dimensions. She stops short of crediting God. I would point to a moment in the winter of '75.

I was 26 and gravely ill. I was coughing up blood and walking down Pico Boulevard in a rainstorm. It was late at night. I was drenched and had no place to sleep. I passed a run of storefronts. One doorknob seemed to glow. I put my hand on it. The door opened effortlessly.

I stepped into a warm office building. I found a stretch of floor near a recessed heating vent. I lay down and fell asleep. My clothes dried during the night. I awoke, revitalized. My bloody coughing fits had abated, temporarily.

God left that door open for me. I have no doubt of that. I was bestowed with moments of reprieve. Other moments have accumulated and have assured my survival.

Invisibility. The miraculous meets the mundane. Moments that build and form states of grace.

I've entered one now. I feel transformed. I'm Beethoven with the late quartets and his hearing restored. Moments form the remainders of lifetimes. I reject this woman as anything less than God's greatest gift to me. I address her with the faith of a lifelong believer. Her very being abrogates all strains of skepticism. She saw me and made me come to her. She found me while I clawed for myself, starved for Her and nobody else. Her great love emboldens me and cuts through my fear and rage. She is an alchemist's casting of Jean Hilliker and something much more. She commands me to step out of the dark and into the light.

A NOTE ABOUT THE TYPE

The text of this book was set in Plantin, a typeface first cut in 1913 by the Monotype Corporation of London. Though the face bears the name of the great Christopher Plantin (ca. 1520–1589), who in the latter part of the sixteenth century owned, in Antwerp, the largest printing and publishing firm in Europe, it is a rather free adaptation of designs by Claude Garamond made for that firm. With its strong, simple lines, Plantin is a no-nonsense face of exceptional legibility.

Composed by North Market Street Graphics,
Lancaster, Pennsylvania

Designed by Virginia Tan

JAMES ELLROY

My Dark Places

On 21 June 1958, Geneva Hilliker Ellroy left her home in California. She was found strangled the next day. Her ten-year-old son James had been with her estranged husband all weekend and was informed of her death on his return. Her murderer was never found, but her death had an enduring effect on her son – he spent his teens and early adult years as a wino, petty burglar and derelict.

Only later, through is obsession with crime fiction, triggered by his mother's murder, did Ellroy begin to delve into his past. Shortly after the publication of his groundbreaking novel *White Jazz*, he determined to return to Los Angeles and, with the help of veteran detective Bill Stoner, attempt to solve the 38-year-old killing.

The result is one of the few classics of crime non-fiction and autobiography to appear in the last few decades; a hypnotic trip to America's underbelly and one man's tortured soul.

JAMES ELLROY

American Tabloid

1958. America is about to emerge into a bright new age – an age that will last until the 1000 days of John F. Kennedy's presidency.

Three men move beneath the glossy surface of power, men allied to the makers and shakers of the era. Pete Bondurant, Howard Hughes's right-hand man, Jimmy Hoffa's hitman; Kemper Boyd – employed by J Edgar Hoover to infiltrate the Kennedy clan; Ward Littell, a man seeking redemption in Bobby Kennedy's drive against organised crime.

The festering discontent of the age that burns brightly in these men's hearts will go into supernova as the Bay of Pigs ends in calamity, the Mob clamours for payback and the 1000 days ends in brutal quietus in 1963.

'Intense and flamboyant ... excellent. The plot runs on high-octane violence ... a powerful book ... one emerges breathless, shaken and ready to change one's view of recent American history'
SUNDAY TELEGRAPH

'A frenetic and explosive thriller ... Ellroy is said to document the "underbelly" of America, but underbelly, my foot. This is the backside, the inside, the blood and the guts'
SUNDAY TIMES

James Ellroy

The Cold Six Thousand

Dallas, November 22nd, 1963. Wayne Tedrow Jr has arrived to kill a man. The fee is $6,000. He finds himself instead in the middle of the cover-up following JFK's assassination. There follows a hellish five-year ride through the sordid underbelly of public policy via Las Vegas, Howard Hughes, Vietnam, CIA dope dealing, Cuba, sleazy showbiz, racism and the Klan.

This is the 1960s under Ellroy's blistering lens, the icons of the era mingled with cops, killers, hoods, and provocateurs. *The Cold Six Thousand* is historical confluence as American nightmare. Fierce, epic fiction. A masterpiece.

'The quality mark of The Cold Six Thousand is that it can give heavyweight punch to even that most worked-over image, the shooting of JKF ...Knockout'
GUARDIAN

'Astonishing ...not America corrupted, but America in its purest, uncut form'
INDEPENDENT

'Richer and darker than ever, this story ...reminds us how far ahead of his peers Ellroy really is'
NEW STATESMAN

'Energetic and enthralling'
SUNDAY TIMES

JAMES ELLROY

Blood's a Rover

It's 1968. Bobby Kennedy and Martin Luther King are dead. The Mob, Howard Hughes and J Edgar Hoover are in a struggle for America's soul, drawing into their murderous conspiracies the damned and the soon-to-be damned.

Wayne Tedrow Jr: parricide, assassin, dope cooker, mouthpiece for all sides, loyal to none. His journey will take him deeper into the darkness.

Dwight Holly: Hoover's enforcer and hellish conspirator in terrible crimes. As Hoover's power wanes, his destiny lurches towards Richard Nixon and self-annihilation.

Don Crutchfield: a kid, a nobody, a wheelman, and a private detective who stumbles upon an ungodly conspiracy from which he and the country may never recover.

All three men are drawn to women on the opposite side of the political and moral spectrum; all are compromised and ripe for destruction.

JAMES ELLROY

The Black Dahlia

'A mesmerising study of psycho-sexual obsession . . . extraordinarily well-written'
THE TIMES

Los Angeles, 15th January 1947: a beautiful young woman walked into the night and met her horrific destiny.

Five days later, her tortured body was found drained of blood and cut in half. The newspapers called her 'The Black Dahlia'. Two cops are caught up in the investigation and embark on a hellish journey that takes them to the core of the dead girl's twisted life.

'A unique voice in American crime writing'
SUNDAY TELEGRAPH

'One of those rare, brilliantly written books you want to press on other people'
TIME OUT

'A wonderful tale of ambition, insanity, passion and deceit'
PUBLISHERS WEEKLY

JAMES ELLROY

White Jazz

'A vivid, enthralling read . . . James Ellroy is the outstanding American crime writer of his generation'
INDEPENDENT

Los Angeles, 1958: a city on the make. A boom town at the edge of a new era ripe for plunder.

Lieutenant Dave Klein: in turn a lawyer, bagman, slum land-lord, mob killer. Klein stands at the centre of a complex web of plots where violence and death will intersect.

'James Ellroy is a genius: the finest American crime writer since Raymond Chandler, and one of the most readable experimental writers in the world'
TIMES LITERARY SUPPLEMENT

'Without him and his crime fiction, there's no David Peace or The Sopranos or Ian Rankin or The Wire or the work of countless writers and film makers who saw a different way of doing things when they first cracked the spine on an Ellroy'
GQ